MANAGING CONTACTS WITH MICROSOFT® OUTLOOK® 2007 BUSINESS CONTACT MANAGER

Edward Kachinske | Stacy Roach | Timothy Kachinske

Course Technology PTR

A part of Cengage Learning

COURSE TECHNOLOGY
CENGAGE Learning™

Australia, Brazil, Japan, Korea, Mexico, Singapore, Spain, United Kingdom, United States

COURSE TECHNOLOGY
CENGAGE Learning™

Managing Contacts with Microsoft Outlook 2007 Business Contact Manager
Edward Kachinske, Stacy Roach, Timothy Kachinske

Publisher and General Manager, Course Technology PTR:
Stacy L. Hiquet

Associate Director of Marketing:
Sarah O'Donnell

Manager of Editorial Services:
Heather Talbot

Marketing Manager:
Jordan Casey

Acquisitions Editor:
Mitzi Koontz

Marketing Assistant:
Adena Flitt

Project Editor:
Jenny Davidson

Technical Reviewer:
Steve Stroz

PTR Editorial Services Coordinator:
Erin Johnson

Interior Layout Tech:
Bill Hartman

Cover Designer:
Mike Tanamachi

Indexer:
Katherine Stimson

Proofreader:
Sandi Wilson

For product information and technology assistance, contact us at
Cengage Learning Customer & Sales Support Center, 1-800-354-9706

For permission to use material from this text or product,
submit all requests online at **cengage.com/permissions**
Further permissions questions can be emailed to
permissionrequest@cengage.com

Microsoft and Outlook are registered trademarks of Microsoft Corporation in the United States and other countries. All other trademarks are the property of their respective owners.

Library of Congress Catalog Card Number: 2007903969

ISBN-13: 978-1-59863-445-7

ISBN-10: 1-59863-445-3

Course Technology
25 Thomson Place
Boston, MA 02210
USA

Cengage Learning is a leading provider of customized learning solutions with office locations around the globe, including Singapore, the United Kingdom, Australia, Mexico, Brazil, and Japan. Locate your local office at:
international.cengage.com/region

Cengage Learning products are represented in Canada by Nelson Education, Ltd.

For your lifelong learning solutions, visit **courseptr.com**

Visit our corporate website at **cengage.com**

Printed in Canada
3 4 5 6 7 11 10 09

For John Abodeely

–EK

For my wife, Carol Gilliland,
and my son, Max Roach.
You both are the light of my life.

–SR

Acknowledgments

This is my 22nd published title and third book with Thomson Course, PTR. It's been a true pleasure working with Stacy Hiquet, Mitzi Koontz, and the whole team at Course, PTR. A big hug goes out to all of you. You really are the best in the business.

This is my second time working with Jenny Davidson as project editor. Jenny's edits, comments, and suggestions are always on target, and the final product is significantly better because of her efforts.

To my Global Services officemates: Courtney Fairchild, Jody Franklin, Matt Thompson, Betty Beimers, and (sometimes) Martin Hicks. It's nice to know that I don't have to go further than the rooftop deck of our office to find happy hour.

My best friend in the industry, Steve Stroz from Gold Coast Advisors in Chicago, agreed to partner up on this project to do the technical edit. Steve's a CRM guru—in products ranging from ACT! to SalesLogix to Microsoft BCM. Steve's wife Kirsten makes every room light up, but their real crowning achievement is their daughter Chloe. At five years old, Chloe is the most articulate young person I've met, and she can name every state capital. Can you?

Many, many thanks to Carol and Max for letting me borrow my co-author Stacy Roach for this project. And to Stacy, one of only a few people who know the acronym HFLCW, you're great.

Oh, and of course—a big shout-out to Susan L.S.B. Luongo from Boston. Mwah!

—EDWARD KACHINSKE

This is my first book, and I could not have done it without the support of my family. My wife, Carol, and our son, Max, fed me, made me laugh, and gave me all the love, support, and encouragement a girl could hope for. And then some—even when I was incredibly cranky.

To the entire team at Thomson Course, PTR, and particularly to Stacy Hiquet and Mitzi Koontz, thanks for the opportunity and all your help and guidance.

As for Jenny Davidson, Ed said working with you would be a joy, and he was right. Thanks for your patient and thoughtful editing and guidance.

There have been many people who have helped me enormously in my career. Too many to mention, but a few need to be called out:

To Ed Solomon, my early mentor and friend, you taught me so much about selling with honesty and integrity—thank you.

To Karen Nickel for your unfailing humor and grace.

To Paul Costanza for your illuminating pontification at any white board, anytime, and even when there wasn't actually a white board present.

To Nancy Yago and Julie Lewis, who I thought were my evil competitors, but turned out to be close colleagues and good friends.

To Susanne McHone for your spot-on and deft management skills; thanks for everything.

As for Liz Hendon and Tami Sauer, your wildly unconditional support, encouragement, and generous gifts of time and knowledge helped me immensely when I started my own business. Your help did a lot to make my success today possible. Not to mention my relative sanity. You two are the best.

And finally, to Edward Kachinske, you are a rock star and I am happy to be your groupie. Thanks for inviting me to write this book with you. As usual, working with you on this project I have learned a ton, had a ball, and would happily do it all over again.

—STACY ROACH

About the Authors

 Edward Kachinske is the author or co-author of 22 titles, including *Managing Contacts with ACT! 2005* and *Managing Contacts with ACT! 2006*, both published by Thomson Course, PTR. Edward has also published more than 100 articles in Customer Relationship Management (CRM) industry journals. Through print journals and electronic publications, more than a half-million people regularly read Edward's articles.

In his ten years in the industry, Edward has been a frequent speaker on contact management subjects. In 2001 Edward started an annual conference, now called Mastering Small Business Consulting. The conference is geared toward CRM consulting firms that target the SMB market. The event attracts hundreds of consulting firm owners each year.

Edward is the president of Innovative Solutions CRM, a firm that helps customers choose and implement contact management solutions. Edward lives and works in Washington, DC.

 Stacy Roach has over 15 years of sales and sales management experience. Her work has primarily been in the technology industry. Stacy has personally relied on contact management tools—including Microsoft Business Contact Manager—to build strong relationships with her clients.

Stacy has authored several articles in CRM industry newsletters. She is a frequent presenter at CRM conferences. Stacy founded an annual conference, now called Mastering Small Business Consulting. The conference is geared toward CRM consulting firms that target the SMB market. The event attracts hundreds of consulting firm owners each year.

Stacy is the president of Power of 3 Consulting, a firm that provides sales consulting and training with a focus on integrating clients' business processes with contact management solutions. Stacy lives and works in the San Francisco Bay area.

Timothy Kachinske has authored more than a dozen titles in the CRM world, including *Managing Contacts with ACT! 2005* and *Managing Contacts with ACT! 2006*. He has published more than 150 industry-related articles, and he works as a contact management consultant.

Timothy lives in a suburb of Washington, DC, with his wife, Judith, and energetic West Highland Terrier, Harry. They have two sons.

 Steve Stroz (Technical Editor) holds multiple technical certifications and is a frequent speaker and instructor at CRM industry conferences throughout North America, Europe, and Australia. In his 16 years as a technology consultant, Steve has served on CRM software product councils, advisory boards, and industry trade associations. During this time, he has authored numerous technical articles and manuals.

Steve is the president of Gold Coast Advisors and resides in Chicago, IL, with his wife, Kirsten, and daughter, Chloe.

Contents

Chapter 6
Managing Your Calendar and Tasks ...63

Chapter 10
Managing Projects 137

Introduction

How to Use This Book

Microsoft Office Outlook 2007 with Business Contact Manager is a great contact management tool aimed primarily at small businesses. Most small businesses we work with rarely have extra time or resources to invest in learning a new application, even one that will help them better manage their relationships with their prospects and clients. So when we designed this book, we weren't expecting anyone to sit down and plow through the thrilling content contained in it from cover to cover. It's not exactly a page-turner. We wrote the book intending that it will be used as a reference tool. You will be able to quickly and easily put your hands on the relevant information that you need and you won't have to sift through lots of verbiage to get there.

The book is divided into chapters, and each chapter is divided into sections. Within each section, you'll find a task. Each page in this book covers a single task, and the tasks make up the bulk of the book.

We have trained users on computer applications for over ten years and have found that people tend to both learn and retain computer skills best when they are hands-on, actually using the application. The tasks in this book are designed to walk you through the different functions of the application, step by step.

What Is Microsoft Office Outlook 2007 with Business Contact Manager?

Microsoft Office Outlook 2007 with Business Contact Manager helps small businesses manage their customer information and interactions, as well as follow up on sales leads and prospects. The contact management functions of Business Contact Manager allow your company to easily track and organize all of the communication history with prospects and clients, including e-mail messages, phone calls, appointments, tasks, notes, and documents. You can also easily share this data with other co-workers.

In addition to the important contact management functionality, Business Contact Manager has three other main areas of functionality—sales opportunity management, marketing campaign management, and project management. Business Contact Manager also includes a dashboard to quickly view the information relevant to your business, as well as reports for analyzing data that are easy to use and customize for your needs. And information from Business Contact Management can easily be exported to Microsoft Excel for further analysis.

Chapter 1

Installing Business Contact Manager

- ◆ Installing and updating Business Contact Manager
- ◆ Managing databases

Installing and updating Business Contact Manager

When you install Outlook 2007, Business Contact Manager is not automatically installed. Business Contact Manager is an add-on for Outlook, and the installation files for Business Contact Manager are stored on a separate CD with the Professional, Small Business, and Ultimate Edition of Office. To use Business Contact Manager, you must first install Outlook 2007 and then install Outlook Business Contact Manager.

Task A   Determining whether Business Contact Manager is already installed on your computer

Business Contact Manager doesn't have a separate icon. It doesn't have its own folder in the Programs part of the Start menu. It lives entirely within Outlook. If you're unsure whether Outlook has the Business Contact Manager components installed, there are a couple spots within Outlook that you can check. If you don't see a Business Contact Manager menu in Outlook, for example, you must install Business Contact Manager.

To determine whether Business Contact Manager is already installed on your computer:

1. Open Outlook.
2. On the menu bar, look for the Business Contact Manager menu. If you see it, you have Business Contact Manager installed.
3. If you don't see a Business Contact Manager menu, click Help in Outlook and look for an About Business Contact Manager for Outlook option. If you don't see it, the Business Contact Manager add-on to Outlook is definitely not installed.

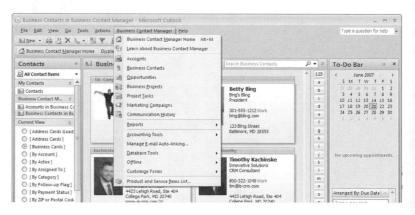

Task B Installing Business Contact Manager

Most editions of Office 2007 (except Basic, Home, Student, and Standard editions) ship with a separate CD that contains Business Contact Manager, Project, Visio, SharePoint, and other components of Office. You'll need to locate this CD to install Business Contact Manager. Keep in mind that the Business Contact Manager install is separate from the actual Outlook install. You must install Outlook before you can install Business Contact Manager.

To install Business Contact Manager:

1. Insert the CD that contains the Business Contact Manager installer. This is most likely not the same CD that you used to install Outlook.
2. Navigate to the Business Contact Manager folder on the CD.
3. Double-click the setup.exe file.
4. Follow the on-screen instructions to load Business Contact Manager onto your computer. The installation should take about ten minutes on current hardware.

Before installing Business Contact Manager, check to make sure Business Contact Manager isn't already installed. If you have a Business Contact Manager menu in Outlook, you will not need to perform these tasks.

Business Contact Manager 2007 only works with Office 2007.

Task C   Checking for updates

From time to time, Microsoft releases updates for most of its software programs, including Outlook and Business Contact Manager. You can update Outlook and Business Contact Manager from Windows Update or right from within the Outlook program.

If you are working in a multi-user database environment, it's a good idea to update all Outlook installations at the same time.

To update your Outlook and Business Contact Manager installations to the latest version:

1. In Outlook, click Help | Check for Updates.
2. Internet Explorer will open and automatically take you to the Windows Update page where you can check for updates. If any are available, you'll be able to download and install them.

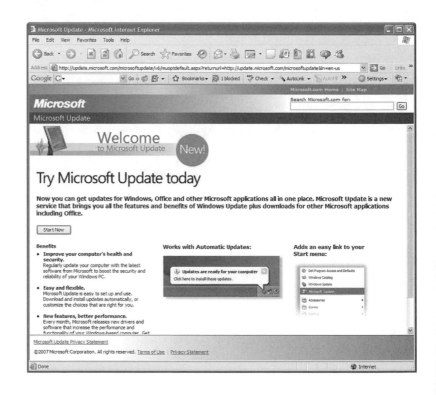

Managing databases

When Business Contact Manager is installed, a database is created for you. You can, however, create additional databases if you want to segregate your data into multiple, independent files. You can create a virtually unlimited number of databases. Data created in Business Contact Manager is stored in the local instance of SQL Server 2005 Express Edition that gets installed when you install Business Contact Manager. You can share a database across the network, but you can only create a database on your local computer.

Task A   Creating a standalone database

To create a new database, you must be on the computer that will store the database. Business Contact Manager databases can only be stored on the local computer. Once you have created a database, you will have the option to share it with other network users.

To create a new database on your computer:

1. Click Business Contact Manager | Database Tools | Create or Select a Database.
2. Choose the Create a new database option.
3. In the Database name field, type the name for your new database.
4. Click Next.

You cannot create two databases with the same name on the same computer.

To open other databases on your local computer or network, click Business Contact Manager | Database Tools | Create or Select a Database. Then choose the Select an existing database option.

Microsoft Office Outlook 2007 with Business Contact Manager

Create or select a Business Contact Manager database
Microsoft Office Outlook 2007 with Business Contact Manager stores information about your business contacts in a database. You can create a new database or select an existing database.

Click one of the following options:

⦿ **Create a new database**
Type a name for your new Business Contact Manager database.
Database name: MSSmallBusiness2

◯ **Select an existing database**
Type the name of the computer where the existing Business Contact Manager database is stored, and then click Connect. If the database is stored on another person's computer, the owner of the database must share the database with you before you can connect to it.

Computer name: KACHINSKE   [Connect]
Database name: MSSmallBusiness   ▾

[Help]   [Next >] [Cancel]

| Task B | **Creating a networked database** |

To create a networked database, you will need to start on the computer that will be used as your server. Create the database if you have not already done so, and then follow these instructions to share the database with other users.

If you are sharing a database on Windows XP or Windows Vista, a maximum of ten people can connect to your database at any time. This limitation does not exist for server-grade operating systems, like Windows Server 2003.

Only a local administrator on the computer hosting the database can share the database with other network users.

To share your database with other users:

1. Create your database on the computer that will act as your server. Make sure this database is open in Business Contact Manager.
2. Click Business Contact Manager | Database Tools | Share Database.
3. Choose the I want to share my data option. Check the option to share data with other users working on other computers in your network. Click Next.
4. Choose an option to either keep or remove your e-mail linking options. Click Next.
5. Select the users that should be able to access the database. You may need to click the Add New User button. Click Next.
6. Review the security settings and click Next.
7. Click Finish.

Share Database

Share Your Business Contact Manager Database

Before you share your database, consider the potential security effects carefully. For more information, click Help.

This Business Contact Manager database is currently: Shared

○ I do not want to share my data

○ I want to share my data

☑ with users working on other computers in my network
Only an administrator on this computer can allow users on other computers to access your data.

Help   Next >   Cancel

Task C   Connecting to an existing database on your network

Before you will be able to connect to an existing database, an administrator on the computer hosting the database must grant you access to it. Detailed instructions for granting access to a database are covered on the preceding page.

To connect to an existing database:

1. Click Business Contact Manager | Database Tools | Create or Select a Database.
2. Choose the Select an existing database option.
3. Type the host computer name in the Computer name field. Click Connect.
4. From the Database name drop-down, choose a database.
5. Click Next.
6. The remote database will be opened.

If you need to know the name of a computer on the Windows network, you can:

- XP: Right-click on My Computer and choose Properties. Click the Computer Name tab to see the name of the computer.
- Vista: Click the Start button. Right-click the Computer option in the right column and choose Properties.
- Command Prompt: Type hostname and press Enter.

Microsoft Office Outlook 2007 with Business Contact Manager

Create or select a Business Contact Manager database
Microsoft Office Outlook 2007 with Business Contact Manager stores information about your business contacts in a database. You can create a new database or select an existing database.

Click one of the following options:

○ **Create a new database**

Type a name for your new Business Contact Manager database.

Database name: MSSmallBusiness2

⊙ **Select an existing database**

Type the name of the computer where the existing Business Contact Manager database is stored, and then click Connect. If the database is stored on another person's computer, the owner of the database must share the database with you before you can connect to it.

Computer name: KACHINSKE   [Connect]

Database name: MSSmallBusiness

[Help]   [Next >]   [Cancel]

Chapter 2

Working with Business Contacts and Accounts

- Working with business contacts
- Working with accounts
- Linking business contacts and accounts
- Adding additional information for accounts and business contacts
- Adding communication history items

Working with business contacts

A database is only as good as the data you've entered. In this section, you'll learn how to add new business contacts to the Business Contact Manager database and enter information about these contacts. When you add a business contact in Outlook, the contact is stored in the Microsoft SQL Server 2005 database that houses your Business Contact Manager data.

Task A   Creating a new business contact

It is very important that you understand the difference between a *contact* and a *business contact* in Outlook. A traditional Outlook *contact* is stored in the same (.pst) file that houses your Inbox and other e-mail folders. A *business contact* is created in the Business Contact Manager component of Outlook and is stored separately in the SQL database for Business Contact Manager. Your Outlook *contacts* do not intermingle with your Business Contact Manager *business contacts*.

To add a new business contact:

1. Go to your list of business contacts. You can get there by clicking Business Contact Manager | Business Contacts.
2. Click Actions | New Business Contact.
3. Enter information about your business contact.
4. Click the Save & Close button.

In Outlook, you have a set of contacts. In Business Contact Manager, you have a set of business contacts. This essentially gives you two sets of contact lists within Outlook. Just know that each time you see references to business contacts, we're talking about the people in your Business Contact Manager database, not your Outlook contacts list.

Task B   Resolving duplicate business contacts

Duplicates are a problem in just about any database. Business Contact Manager makes it hard to enter a duplicate contact by checking—each time you add a new business contact—to see if the business contact already exists. If a duplicate match is found, Business Contact Manager will prompt you for action.

To see how Business Contact Manager deals with duplicate contacts:

1. Go to your list of business contacts. You can get there by clicking Business Contact Manager | Business Contacts.
2. Find an existing contact record and pay attention to the business contact's name.
3. Click Actions | New Business Contact.
4. Enter a new business contact into the database with exactly the same name as the existing business contact. Business Contact Manager will prompt you to either combine your new business contact with the existing duplicate or add the duplicate as a separate contact.

When checking for duplicates, Business Contact Manager is quite literal. If John Doe already exists in your database, attempting to add John P. Doe will not flag the new contact as a duplicate.

BCM compares the Contact and/or E-mail fields when checking for duplicates. You can set options for checking duplicates in Tools | Options | Contact Options.

A duplicate item has been detected

The name or e-mail address of this Business Contact already exists in this folder: Business Contacts

Would you like to:
- ○ Add this as a new Business Contact anyway
- ◉ Update and open the existing Business Contact with new information from this one:

Roach, Stacy (stacy@po3inc.com)

Help   Open Business Contact...   OK   Cancel

When you delete an item in Business Contact Manager, the item is generally not actually deleted. Deleted contacts, accounts, and other items can be restored within the Deleted Items folder.

When you delete an account, business contacts associated with the account are also deleted. In general, Business Contact Manager will usually delete linked items when the parent item is deleted.

Task C   Deleting a business contact

Deleting an unwanted contact is just as simple as adding a new one. Anyone who can access your database will be able to delete a contact. In fact, they could delete every contact in the database.

To delete a business contact:

1. Go to your list of business contacts. You can get there by clicking Business Contact Manager | Business Contacts.
2. Highlight the contact you'd like to delete.
3. Click Edit | Delete or press the Delete key on your keyboard.
4. The contact is automatically moved to the Deleted Items folder.

Microsoft Office Outlook

⚠ This item has been changed. Are you sure you want to delete it?

[Yes]   [No]

Task D   Restoring a deleted business contact

If you accidentally delete a business contact, you can restore the deleted
contact from the Deleted Items folder. Deleted business contacts behave the
same way deleted e-mails behave in Outlook. They aren't actually deleted but
are just sent to a folder pending final deletion.

To restore a deleted contact:

1. Click the Business Contact Manager Home button on the toolbar.
2. On the left side of the screen, click the Business Contact Manager Deleted
   Items folder. It's probably at the bottom of your list of mail folders.
3. Click the contact you'd like to restore.
4. Click Edit | Move to Folder and move the item to your Business Contacts
   folder.

To permanently delete a contact from
Business Contact Manager, just
delete it from the Deleted Items
folder. Once an item has been deleted
from the Deleted Items folder, you
will not be able to recover it.

You can also accomplish most of
these tasks by right-clicking within
the Business Contact Manager
interface.

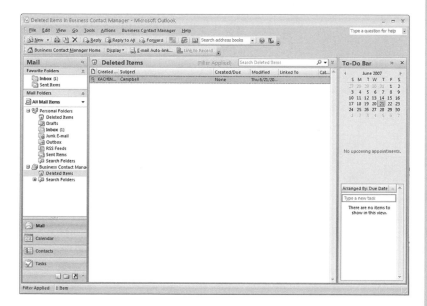

Working with accounts

In addition to the contact entity, Business Contact Manager offers an additional record type—the account. Think of accounts as companies in your database. Business contacts can be associated with these accounts. Linking your business contacts with accounts lets you create an account-centric database system with Business Contact Manager.

Task A   Creating a new account

Adding a new account to the database entails the same general process you use to add a new business contact. You should probably go into one of the account views before adding a new account, and it's a good idea to check to see if an account already exists before adding one to your database.

To create a new account from scratch:

1. Go to your list of accounts. You can get there by clicking Business Contact Manager | Accounts.
2. Click Actions | New Account.
3. Enter information about your account.
4. Click the Save & Close button to save your changes and return to Business Contact Manager.

From any of your account views, you can right-click within the list of accounts and choose the option to create a new account.

Task B   Creating a new account from an existing business contact

If you've already added a business contact to your Business Contact Manager database, you can easily create an account using the contact information in your business contact. Doing this saves you the trouble of having to add the same address twice.

To create a new account from a business contact:

1. Go to your list of business contacts. You can get there by clicking Business Contact Manager | Business Contacts.
2. Open a business contact. The easiest way to do this is to double-click it from one of the business contact views.
3. Under the Linked account header, click the Account button.
4. Click the New button.
5. A new account record appears. You'll notice that basic contact information—like the address and phone number—are carried over from the business contact.
6. Click the Save & Close button.

Creating an account from an existing business contact automatically links the business contact with the account record.

Task C   Deleting an account

Removing an account from your database follows the same general process you'd follow to delete any other database entity. In addition to the steps outlined on this page, you can right-click on an account in any of the account views and choose the Delete option. You can also press the Delete key while an account is highlighted to remove it from the database.

Be careful! Deleting an account also deletes all business contacts associated with the contact.

To delete an account:

1. Go to your list of accounts. You can get there by clicking Business Contact Manager | Accounts.
2. Highlight the account you'd like to delete.
3. Click Edit | Delete.
4. The account is automatically moved to the Deleted Items folder.

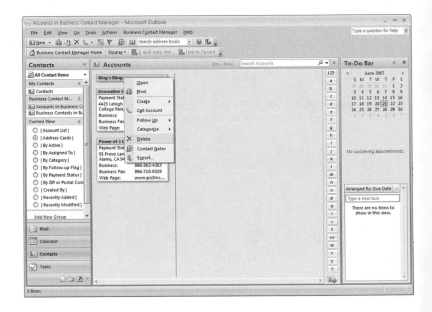

Task D   Restoring a deleted account

After deleting an account, both the account and the business contacts associated with the account are deleted. If you accidentally delete an account, Business Contact Manager can automatically undelete both the account and the associated business contacts in one step.

To restore an account:

1. Click Business Contact Manager | Business Contact Manager Home to get to the home screen.
2. On the left, locate and click the Deleted Items folder under the Business Contact Manager main folder.
3. Highlight the account you'd like to undelete.
4. Click Edit | Move to Folder.
5. Choose the Accounts folder and click OK.
6. Both the account and any associated business contacts will be restored.

You can restore multiple accounts at once. Just highlight all of the accounts you'd like to restore from the Deleted Items folder, and click Edit | Move to Folder to move them all to your Accounts folder.

Linking business contacts and accounts

Business Contact Manager provides a one-to-many relationship between accounts and contacts. In other words, you could have XYZ Company in your database as an account. Everyone who works for XYZ could be entered as a business contact, and all of these business contacts could be linked with the parent company. When you are looking at the details for any account, it's easy to see a list of the business contacts that have been associated with that account, and linking business contacts with accounts makes it easy to run account-centric reports.

Task A   Linking business contacts with accounts

This task assumes that you already have a business contact and an account in your database. For situations where you do not have both, check out the other tasks in this section that cover how to create an account from a business contact.

To link an existing business contact with an account:

1. Go to your list of business contacts. You can get there by clicking Business Contact Manager | Business Contacts.
2. Double-click the business contact that you'd like to associate with an account.
3. Under the Linked account header, click the Account button.
4. Choose an account, and click the Link To button. It's important here that you do not click OK. You must click the Link To button.
5. Once you've clicked the Link To button, click OK to exit the dialog box.
6. Click the Save & Close button.

Task B Removing the link between a business contact and an account

If you no longer want to associate a business contact with an account, removing the link is easy. In fact, you can re-associate a business contact with a new account in the same step. This is especially useful if someone leaves a company and joins another in your database.

To remove the business contact/account link:

1. Go to your list of business contacts. You can get there by clicking Business Contact Manager | Business Contacts.
2. Double-click the business contact that you'd like to associate with an account.
3. Under the Linked account header, click the Account button.
4. To the right of the Link To button, highlight the account name and press the Delete key.
5. Click OK.
6. Click the Save & Close button.

Linked Records

Link To ->	Power of 3 Consulting

Removing the link between a business contact and an account does not delete the business contact or the account. It simply disassociates the two database entities from each other.

Adding additional information for accounts and business contacts

For the most part, entering data into a Business Contact Manager database is fairly easy. When a field appears on the screen, you click in the field, enter text, and click a button to save the changes. In this section, we'll point out a few spots where you can enter extended data for a business contact.

Task A   Specifying the first, middle, and last name for a business contact

When you are entering a business contact into Business Contact Manager, you'll notice that there is only one field for the contact's name. However, Business Contact Manager actually stores the data in five separate fields: Title, First, Middle, Last, and Suffix. When entering business contacts, it's important to make sure these components of the name are flagged correctly.

To specify the first, middle, and last name:

1. Go to your list of business contacts. You can get there by clicking Business Contact Manager | Business Contacts.
2. Double-click one of your existing business contacts.
3. To the left of the Full Name field, click the Full Name button.
4. Specify the title, first, middle, last, and suffix components of the name.

Why is this important? Let's say the last name of a business contact isn't flagged correctly. When you include this person in a marketing campaign, you might set the salutations for your letter templates to show the title and the last name. In this sort of situation, having an incorrectly flagged name will make your letters look like poorly planned form letters.

Task B   Adding a picture for a business contact

If you're a visual person, it might help to have a picture of your business contact appear when viewing the person's record. If you have the picture in a standard image format, like a JPG, GIF, or PNG file, it's easy to associate the photo with the business contact. Photos appear when editing the business contact, and they also appear when looking at the business card view.

To associate a picture with a business contact:

1. Go to your list of business contacts. You can get there by clicking Business Contact Manager | Business Contacts.
2. Double-click an existing business contact.
3. Under the Internet header, locate the picture icon. It's to the left of the E-mail field. Click the picture icon.
4. Locate and double-click the image file you'd like to associate with the business contact.
5. Click the Save & Close button.

If your image is too large to fit on the business card or within the image area on the business contact editing dialog box, Business Contact Manager will automatically resize it to fit within the space provided.

Task C   Adding additional field information for a business contact

While you are editing a business contact, most fields appear and are editable right within the business contact editing dialog box. However, there are a couple hidden spots where you can keep additional information for a business contact.

To view all field areas for a business contact:

1. Go to your list of business contacts. You can get there by clicking Business Contact Manager | Business Contacts.

2. Double-click an existing business contact.

3. In the Show section of the ribbon, look at the different editing views. Right now, you're in the General view.

4. Click the Details view. Take a moment to look at the fields available in this view.

5. Click the User-Defined Fields view. If you have customized any fields in your Business Contact Manager database, they will appear in this view. Adding customized fields is covered in Chapter 12.

6. Click the Save & Close button.

Depending on your screen resolution, it may help to maximize the business contact editing dialog box. This will make it easier to see all of the icons on the ribbon.

Adding communication history items

One of the most powerful features of Business Contact Manager is its ability to track communication history items for business contacts, accounts, opportunities, and business projects. Communication history items provide a way of tracking notes, phone logs, opportunities, projects, tasks, e-mail messages, appointments, and files. Looking for a chronological list of everything you've done with a business contact, account, opportunity, or business project? Go to the Communication History view.

Task A — Viewing communication history items for a record

All of the steps in this section apply to business contacts, accounts, opportunities, and business projects. All of these database entities have communication history items.

To view communication history items for a record:

1. For this example, we'll assume that you are viewing a communication history item for a business contact; however, the steps for viewing communication history items for other database entities are the same.
2. Double-click the business contact to open it for editing.
3. In the Show group of the ribbon, click the History view.
3. Look at the communication history items for your record. By default, they are sorted in chronological order, but you can change the sort by clicking the View drop-down at the top of the list.
4. Close the business contact to return to Business Contact Manager.

Types of communication history items that can be added for a business contact:

- Business Note
- Phone Log
- Opportunity
- Business Project
- Task
- Mail Message
- Appointment
- File

Task B   Inserting a business note

Once you've entered a business contact into Business Contact Manager, you might find it useful to be able to add notes for that contact. You can add an unlimited number of business notes for any business contact, and each note can be as long as you require. Business notes in Business Contact Manager are a type of communication history item.

To add a business note for a business contact:

1. Go to your list of business contacts. You can get there by clicking Business Contact Manager | Business Contacts.

2. Highlight an existing business contact.

3. Click Actions | Create | New Business Note for Business Contact. You could also right-click a business contact and select Create | New Business Note for Business Contact.

4. Give your note a subject, and enter the body of the note in the Comments section.

5. Click Save & Close to exit the note, and click Save & Close again to return to Business Contact Manager.

This task shows you how to enter a note for a business contact. However, you can use the same process to add notes for accounts, opportunities, and business projects. All of these database entities can have notes attached.

This page shows you how to add a business note. It's important to understand that business notes are different from notes. Notes are kept in Outlook and aren't attached to a contact. Business notes are kept in Business Contact Manager and are attached to a contact, activity, opportunity, or business project.

Task C Linking a file

You can attach any file on your hard drive or network to a business contact, account, opportunity, or business project. Files that have been linked to a contact are only available for users who have access to the original file. In other words, if you link a file from your My Documents folder, that document won't be accessible to other Business Contact Manager users on your network.

To link a file to a business contact:

1. Go to your list of business contacts. You can get there by clicking Business Contact Manager | Business Contacts.
2. Double-click an existing business contact.
3. In the Show section of the ribbon, click the History view.
4. Click the New button and choose the File option.
5. Browse to the file you'd like to link and double-click it.
6. The file is now linked to the business contact.

You could also right-click on a business contact and choose Create | New Linked File for Business Contact. You can use this method to add other types of Communication History entries for a business contact as well.

Task D   Using the Communication History view

The Communication History view shows a big picture listing of all communication history items that have been added to your Business Contact Manager database. You can sort this view by type, subject, linked record, date, and record creator. The look and feel of the Communication History view should be familiar if you use Outlook for e-mail.

Click View | Autopreview to automatically see the first few lines of each communication history item within the Communication History view.

For more detailed searching options in the Communication History view, click the chevron icon (☒) to the right of the search field to bring up the Query Builder.

To view all communication history items entered recently:

1. Click Business Contact Manager | Communication History.
2. The Communication History view appears.
3. To search for a specific item within the Communication History view, click in the search field in the upper-right corner of the view.
4. To sort by any field currently showing, click once on the column header. Click again to sort in the opposite order.

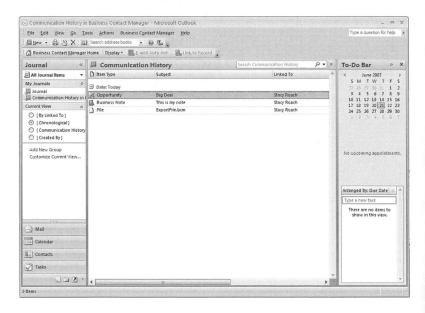

Chapter 3

Viewing Your Data

- Business Contact Manager Home
- Understanding views
- Customizing your views

Business Contact Manager Home

After Business Contact Manager has been installed, Outlook will show an extra toolbar with a Business Contact Manager Home button prominently displayed. Clicking this Business Contact Manager button will take you (from whatever screen you're currently viewing in Outlook) directly to the Business Contact Manager Home screen. From the Business Contact Manager Home screen, you can access accounts, business contacts, opportunities, business projects, project tasks, and marketing campaigns.

Task A   Getting to the Business Contact Manager Home screen

The easiest way to get to the Business Contact Manager Home screen is to click the Business Contact Manager Home button on the toolbar, but you can also get to the Home screen from the Business Contact Manager menu.

To get to the Business Contact Manager Home screen:

1. From anywhere in Outlook, click the Business Contact Manager Home button on the toolbar.
2. Alternatively, you can click Business Contact Manager | Business Contact Manager Home, or press Alt + M.
3. The Business Contact Manager Home screen should appear.

If you don't see a Business Contact Manager Home button on the toolbar, you might not have Outlook Business Contact Manager installed.

If you have Business Contact Manager installed but don't see a Business Contact Manager Home button on the toolbar, right-click the toolbar and choose the Customize option. Make sure the Business Contact Manager for Outlook toolbar is checked.

Task B Options in the Business Contact Manager Home screen

The Business Contact Manager Home screen is customizable, and you can use it as your launching point for performing tasks within Business Contact Manager.

To view all of the options in the Business Contact Manager Home screen:

1. Click the Business Contact Manager Home button on the toolbar to get to the Business Contact Manager Home screen.
2. In the upper-right corner of the Business Contact Manager Home screen, click the Add or Remove Content option.
3. The Add or Remove Content dialog box appears, and you can use this dialog box to add new items or remove existing items from the Business Contact Manager Home screen.
4. Click OK to save your changes.

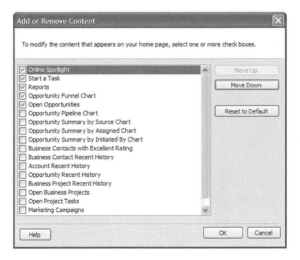

We devote an entire chapter to the Business Contact Manager Home screen in this book. Check out Chapter 12 for detailed information on customizing the Business Contact Manager Home screen.

Task C   Using the Business Contact Manager menu

After Business Contact Manager has been installed, you'll notice an extra Business Contact Manager menu in Outlook. You'll find the Business Contact Manager menu between Actions and Help. If you need a quick way to switch between different parts of Business Contact Manager, this menu is probably the easiest way. For example, if you need to quickly look at your business contacts, you can get right to them from the Business Contact Manager menu.

To use the Business Contact Manager menu:

1. Click Business Contact Manager on the menu.
2. Take a moment to look at the options on the Business Contact Manager menu.
3. You can easily go to views that display account, business contact, opportunity, business project, project task, marketing campaign, and communication history data.

From the Business Contact Manager menu, you can also run reports and perform database maintenance tasks—like offline database setup, backup, and customization.

Understanding views

Before you can really effectively use Business Contact Manager, you'll need to have a good understanding of how to get to the data. In this section, you'll learn how to view most of your basic database items—like accounts, business contacts, and opportunities.

Task A   Navigating through the standard views

Unlike with most contact managers, Business Contact Manager spreads contact and customer management features throughout the product. They're not really in a central spot. Business contacts and accounts can be viewed in the Contacts area of Outlook. Business projects and marketing campaigns are viewed in Outlook's tasks area. What brings all of this together is the Business Contact Manager menu item, where you can access any view.

To navigate through the standard views:

1. Locate the Outlook Navigation Pane. It's in the lower-left corner of Outlook, and it contains the Mail, Calendar, Contacts, Tasks, and a few other icons.
2. In the Outlook Navigation Pane, click the Contacts button. Above the Navigation Pane, you should see a group that contains Accounts and Business Contacts in Business Contact Manager.
3. In the Outlook Navigation Pane, click the Tasks button. Above the Navigation Pane, you should see Business Contact Manager opportunities, marketing campaigns, business projects, and project tasks.
4. Now, click the Business Contact Manager option on the menu. You should see all of your Business Contact Manager views available through this central interface.

From the Business Contact Manager menu, you can access:
- Accounts
- Business Contacts
- Opportunities
- Business Projects
- Project Tasks
- Marketing Campaigns
- Communication History

Task B   Viewing business contacts

If you just want to see a list of your business contacts, you can get to this list from the Contacts area in Outlook. It's important to understand the difference between Outlook contacts and Business Contact Manager contacts. Contacts in Outlook are not stored in your Business Contact Manager database.

To view a list of your business contacts:

1. Click Business Contact Manager | Business Contacts.
2. A list of your business contacts will appear.
3. On the left, take a look at the Current View group. Within this group, take a look at the various views.
4. Click each view to see the various ways that the business contacts can be displayed.

Click the Customize Current view option at the bottom of the list of views to customize the look and feel of the business contacts view you're in.

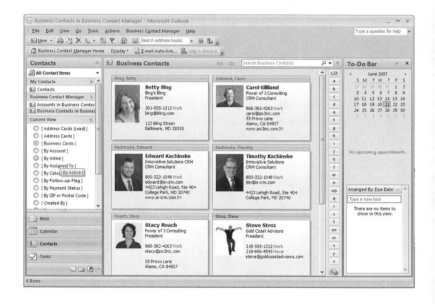

Task C Viewing accounts

Looking at account data pretty much follows the same steps you take to view contact data. There is an option to view account data on the Business Contact Manager menu, and Accounts in Business Contact Manager is one of the options in Outlook's Contacts area.

To view a list of your accounts:

1. Click Business Contact Manager | Accounts.
2. A list of account data from your Business Contact Manager database appears.
3. On the left side of the Outlook interface, take a look at the Current View group. Notice the view that you're currently showing. Try changing the view, and cycle through the different views to see the various ways that account data can be viewed.

Check out the Address Cards view in the list of views on the left side of the screen. This view will be very familiar if you've used previous versions of Outlook to manage contacts.

Task D   Viewing opportunities

Opportunity data is classified under the Tasks area in Outlook. In the Navigation Pane (in the lower-left corner of Outlook) click the Tasks button. Further up in the same column, you should see a number of Business Contact Manager data types, including your opportunities.

Chapter 7 is devoted to opportunity management in this book. In that chapter, you can find out how to add an opportunity, and you'll learn how to track that opportunity as it goes through your sales process.

To view a list of your opportunities:

1. Click Business Contact Manager | Opportunities.
2. A list of the opportunities in your database appears.
3. On the left side of the Outlook interface, take a look at the Current View group. Try changing the view, and cycle through the different views to see the various ways that opportunity data can be viewed.

Task E   Viewing communication history

As you work with business contacts, accounts, opportunities, and other database items, you can add communication history items for each database item. So, you may have a note that is relevant to a specific opportunity. Or you may have a file that you'd like to link to a specific business contact. Collectively, these communication history items can be viewed in the Communication History view.

To view communication history items:

1. Click Business Contact Manager | Communication History.
2. A list of communication history items added to the database will appear.
3. On the left side of the screen, you can choose to view the communication history items by linked database item, chronologically, or by user.

Types of communication history items that show in the communication history view are:

- Business Notes
- Phone logs
- Opportunities
- Business Projects
- Tasks
- E-mail Messages
- Appointments
- Linked Files

Customizing your views

So far in this chapter, you've learned how to view different types of database items—like business contacts, accounts, and opportunities. One of the things you'll notice about each of these database items is that they all have multiple views. You can view your business contacts in business card format, or you can see them in a spreadsheet-like phone list view. Each of these views is customizable.

Task A Customizing the views

Throughout this section, we'll show you how to customize views. Keep in mind that these instructions are, for the most part, valid for all of the database items in Business Contact Manager: business contacts, accounts, opportunities, business projects, marketing campaigns, and communication history items.

To customize a view:

The rest of the chapter shows specifically how to customize parts of a view. If this page interests you, check out the next few, as well.

1. Go to the view that you would like to customize. For example, if you would like to customize the Address Cards view for your business contacts, you'd click Business Contact Manager | Business Contacts. Then, you'd choose the Address Cards view from the list of views on the left.
2. At the bottom of the list of views, you'll see an option to customize the current view. Click Customize Current View.
3. In the Customize View dialog box, you can edit the fields that are displayed on the view, the default sort, the filter, and other settings.
4. Click the Reset Current View button to reset the view settings to the installation default.
5. Click OK to save your changes.

Task B   Changing the default sort for a view

Many of the spreadsheet-like views for business contacts, accounts, opportunities, and other database items have a default sort. You can change this default sort, and then each time you go into the view, you'll see the data sorted just the way you want.

To change the default sort for a view:

1. Go to the view that you would like to customize. For example, if you would like to customize the By Assigned To view for opportunities, you'd click Business Contact Manager | Opportunities. Then, you'd choose the By Assigned To view from the list of views on the left.
2. Click the Customize Current View option at the bottom of the list of views.
3. Click the Sort button.
4. Choose up to four fields for your sort. For example, you could sort by priority instead of opportunity title, which is the default.
5. Click OK twice to return to the list of opportunities.

This specific example works for opportunities, but you can also change the default sort for business contacts, accounts, business projects, and other database items. Follow the same steps, but instead of starting in an Opportunities view, start in a view for the database item you'd like to customize.

Task C   Changing the fields that show in a view

By default, the Phone List view for business contacts shows about ten fields. However, if you'd like to see more fields in this view, adding them is easy. Like other tasks in this chapter, these instructions for adding fields to a view transfer to most business contact, account, opportunity, and other database item views.

To customize views:

1. Go to the view that you would like to customize. For example, if you would like to customize the Phone List view for your business contacts, you'd click Business Contact Manager | Business Contacts. Then, you'd choose the Phone List view from the list of views on the left.

2. Click the Customize Current View option at the bottom of the list of views.

3. Click the Fields button.

4. Set the maximum number of lines that can be devoted to any business contact in the drop-down at the top of the screen.

5. In the middle part of the Show Fields dialog box, you'll see two lists of contacts. Fields not currently showing are in the list on the left. Fields that are currently showing are in the list on the right.

6. To add a field to the view, highlight it from the list on the left. Click the Add button.

7. Click OK twice to save your changes.

Need to add a field that isn't currently in the database? Click the New Field button in the Show Fields dialog box to add the field to your Business Contact Manager database.

Task D   Changing conditional font size for items in a view

This feature is a bit hard to find within Business Contact Manager, but it is extremely powerful. You can create conditional formatting rules for contacts. So, for example, you might want your high priority opportunities to display in a red font. Set the condition on your view, and from that point forward, high priority opportunities will stand out.

To set conditional formatting on a view:

1. Go to the view that you would like to customize. For example, if you would like to customize the By Assigned To view for opportunities, you'd click Business Contact Manager | Opportunities. Then, you'd choose the By Assigned To view from the list of views on the left.
2. Click the Customize Current View option at the bottom of the list of views.
3. Click the Automatic Formatting button.
4. Click the Add button to create a new rule.
5. Click the Font button to specify the font attributes for opportunities that match the rule.
6. Click the Condition button to specify the filter. Go to the Advanced tab to set a query.
7. When your filter is set, click OK twice to return to the list of opportunities.

This specific example works for opportunities, but you can also change the default sort for business contacts, accounts, business projects, and other database items. Follow the same steps, but instead of starting in an Opportunities view, start in a view for the database item you'd like to customize.

Chapter 4

Categorizing Business Contacts, Accounts, and Opportunities

- Creating and editing categories
- Categorizing database items

Creating and editing categories

From time to time, you'll want to associate certain otherwise unrelated business contacts, accounts, or opportunities. Business Contact Manager's category feature lets you do this. With categories, you can make temporary or permanent associations of database items. You can then easily view just business contacts in a certain category, just opportunities in another category, and so on.

Task A   Creating a new category

Out of the box, Business Contact Manager has a number of pre-defined categories. There's a red category, and a blue category, and a number of other activities named after colors. Beyond the color categories, though, you can create additional categories for things like holiday card lists and hot prospects.

To create a new category:

1. Go to one of the Business Contact Manager views. For example, you could go to a list of business contacts.
2. Click Edit | Categorize | All Categories. The Color Categories dialog box appears.
3. Click the New button.
4. Type the name of your new category. Assign it a color and shortcut key, if needed.
5. Click OK twice to return to Business Contact Manager.

Instead of clicking Edit | Categorize, you can click the Category button on the toolbar. It's the one that looks like four multi-colored squares.

Task B Editing an existing category

Business Contact Manager comes with a number of pre-defined categories, each named after a color. You might want to rename these. You might want to edit a category that you created previously. Editing an existing category is as easy as creating a new one.

To edit an existing category:

1. Go to one of the Business Contact Manager views. For example, you could go to a list of accounts.
2. Click Edit | Categorize | All Categories. The Color Categories dialog box appears.
3. Highlight the category you'd like to edit.
4. Click the Rename button to rename the category.
5. Use the Color and Shortcut Key drop-downs to change attributes for the category.
6. Click OK to return to Business Contact Manager.

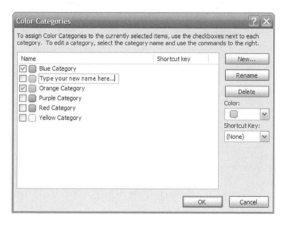

Task C   Deleting a category

If you no longer need a category, you can delete it. Deleting a category with the instructions in this task will remove the category from the master category list; however, if you want to permanently remove the category, you will have to make sure no existing database items are included in the deleted category.

Deleting a category doesn't remove the category from any existing business contacts.

To delete a category:

1. Go to one of the Business Contact Manager views. For example, you could go to a list of accounts.
2. Click Edit | Categorize | All Categories. The Color Categories dialog box appears.
3. Highlight the category you'd like to delete.
4. Click the Delete button. Confirm the deletion by clicking Yes.
5. Click OK.

Microsoft Office Outlook

⚠ Are you sure you want to delete the category "Green Category"? Deleting this category removes it from your category list but does not affect your previously categorized items.

[Yes]   [No]

Task D   Setting the Quick Click category

If there is a category that you use often, you can set a Quick Click category. When you assign a category to the Quick Click feature, clicking the Categories column for any database item will automatically add the item to the set category.

To set the Quick Click category:

1. Go to one of the Business Contact Manager views. For example, you could go to a list of opportunities.
2. Click Edit | Categorize | Set Quick Click.
3. From the drop-down, choose the category that you would like to assign to the Quick Click column.
4. Click OK.

In any of the list views, you can right-click on the column headers and select the Field Chooser option to add the Categories column. It's not on most views by default.

Categorizing database items

You can add an unlimited number of database items (like business contacts, accounts, or opportunities) to a category. Any database item can be a member of some or all of your categories.

Task A	**Categorizing new business contacts, accounts, or opportunities**

It's easy to categorize a new business contact, account, or opportunity while you are creating the database item.

These instructions work for business contacts, accounts, opportunities, and business projects.

To categorize a new business contact (or other database item):

1. Create a new business contact.
2. In the Business Contact dialog box, enter the basic details for your business contact.
3. In the Options section of the ribbon, click the Categorize button.
4. Choose a category.
5. Click Save & Close to save your changes.

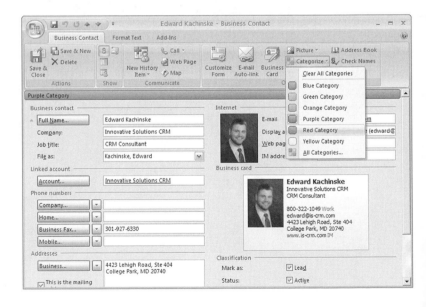

Task B Categorizing existing business contacts, accounts, or opportunities

With just a couple clicks, you can add any database item to a category. Adding a business contact, account, or opportunity to a category can be done from the Edit menu, and it can also be done with two clicks on the toolbar.

To categorize an existing business contact (or other database item):

1. Highlight a business contact, account, opportunity, or other database item.
2. Click Edit | Categorize, and choose a category for the database item.

After clicking Edit | Categorize, choose the All Categories option if you don't see your category in the list. The quick list only shows the first dozen or so categories.

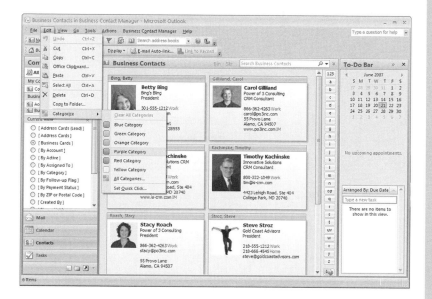

You could also filter any view to just show business contacts, accounts, or opportunities in a specific category. Just right-click in the list view and choose the Filter option. In the More Choices tab, choose a category.

Right-clicking on an actual record won't give you the option to filter. Right-clicking anywhere else on the view *will* allow you to set a filter.

Task C   Viewing database items by category

When you're looking at accounts or business contacts, one of the standard views shows your accounts and business contacts by category.

To view business contacts (or other database items) by category:

1. Click Business Contact Manager | Business Contacts to bring up a list of business contacts.
2. On the left side of the Business Contact Manager interface, locate the list of views.
3. Switch to the [By Category] view.
4. A list of your business contacts will appear, grouped by category.

Task D   Removing category assignment

Removing a category assignment for a business contact, account, or opportunity follows the exact same process you took to add the database item to the category.

To remove category assignment for a business contact (or other database item):

1. Click Business Contact Manager | Business Contacts to bring up a list of business contacts.
2. Click Edit | Categorize, and click the category. This will toggle category assignment for the business contact.

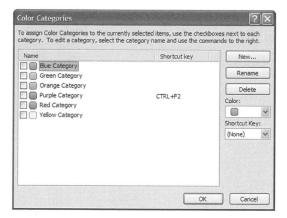

Click Edit | Categorize | All Categories to see a list of all category assignments for the database item (contact, account, or opportunity) that is currently highlighted. In this interface, you'll see a checkbox next to each category.

Chapter 5

Finding Your Data

- Simple searches
- Using the Query Builder
- Applying filters
- Working with Search Folders

Simple searches

Business Contact Manager makes it easy to find your contact data. Need a person's phone number? No matter where you are within Outlook, it's only a couple clicks away. This section focuses on running simple searches—finding a contact by his or her last name, for example. Later in this chapter, we'll cover more complex queries.

Task A   Finding a business contact

From within any of the business contact views, you can search for a business contact. In the upper-right corner of all business contact views, you'll see a search bar. This search bar is used to locate specific business contacts.

To locate a specific business contact:

1. Click Business Contact Manager | Business Contacts to bring up a list of business contacts.
2. In the upper-right corner of the view, locate the search bar. By default, this search bar says Search Contacts within the field, but that text goes away when you click in the field.
3. Click in the search bar and type part of your business contact's name. This could be a first name, company name, last name, etc.
4. Press the magnifying glass icon (or press Enter) to execute the search.

After running a search, the orange bar at the top of the Business Contacts view will display (Search Results) to indicate that you are only looking at a subset of the database.

Press the red X icon to the right of the search bar to clear your search results and return to showing all business contacts in your view.

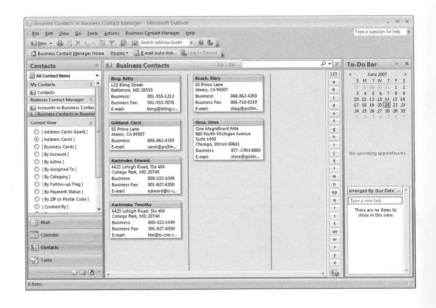

Task B   Finding an account

Finding an account follows the same general steps required to find a business contact; however, you'll perform these steps within one of the account views. When searching for an account, you will use the search bar in the upper-right corner of the account views.

To find a specific account:

1. Click Business Contact Manager | Accounts to bring up a list of accounts.
2. In the upper-right corner of the view, locate the search bar. By default, this search bar says Search Accounts within the field, but that text goes away when you click in the field.
3. Click in the search bar and type part of the name of the account you are trying to find.
4. Click the magnifying button to the right of the search bar to execute the search.
5. Click the red X icon to the right of the search bar to cancel the search and return to showing all accounts in your view.

When searching for an account, you don't have to know the full name of the account. For example, if you are looking for ABC Corporation, you could enter ABC in the search bar.

You can do similar simple searches for opportunities. Just go to one of the opportunity views, and you'll see a search bar in the upper-right corner.

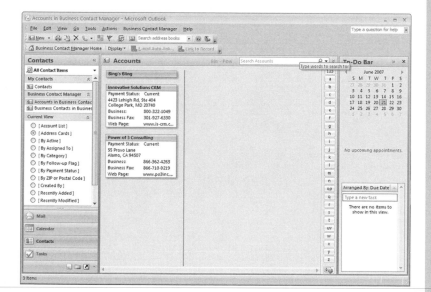

Task C Specifying simple search options

When you are performing a simple search for a contact, you'll notice a drop-down on the right side of the search bar. This drop-down lets you specify some simple search options for finding business contacts, accounts, or opportunities.

To see the simple search options:

1. Click Business Contact Manager on the menu and select to go into Accounts, Business Contacts, or Opportunities.
2. Once you are looking at your accounts, business contacts, or opportunities, locate the search bar. It's in the bar in the upper-right corner of your view. (The bar is probably orange.)
3. Click the drop-down to the right of the search bar and choose Search Options.
4. In the Search Options dialog box, you can specify a number of search options, including search result highlighting.
5. Click OK to return to Business Contact Manager.

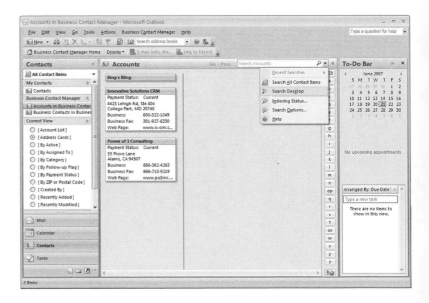

Using the Query Builder

The Query Builder is one of the most powerful features within Business Contact Manager, but it's also one of the hardest to find. The Query Builder lets you search for specific values in one or more fields at once to find the records you're looking for.

Task A · Opening the Query Builder

The Query Builder is available in all of the Business Contact Manager views: Accounts, Business Contacts, Opportunities, Business Projects, Project Tasks, Marketing Campaigns, and Communication History. Opening the Query Builder in any of these views follows the same general process.

To locate and open the Query Builder:

1. Go to any of your Business Contact Manager views (Accounts, Business Contacts, Opportunities, etc.).
2. In the upper-right corner, locate the search bar. To the right of the search bar, you'll see a chevron (☑). Click this.
3. The Query Builder will expand at the top of your view. The Query Builder should show you a half-dozen or so fields that you can use for a specific search.

Click the chevron (☑) again to hide the Query Builder in any view.

Task B Finding database items using the Query Builder

You can use the Query Builder to find specific subsets of your business contact, account, opportunity, and other data. The Query Builder lets you search for multiple fields at once. Think of it as an easy interface to create an advanced query.

Click the X to the right of the search bar to clear the search results.

To find business contacts, accounts, opportunities, or other database items using the Query Builder:

1. Go to any of your Business Contact Manager views (Accounts, Business Contacts, Opportunities, etc.).
2. In the upper-right corner, locate the search bar. To the right of the search bar, you'll see a chevron (⌄). Click this icon to bring up the Query Builder.
3. A list of fields appears. Type a value into any of these fields.
4. Click the magnifying glass icon on the right side of the search bar (in the upper-right corner of the Query Builder) to execute the search.

Task C   Modifying fields in the Query Builder

By default, each of the Business Contact Manager views shows a half dozen or so fields that you can use in a query. However, there are many more fields in the Business Contact Manager database. It's easy to modify the fields that display in the Query Builder.

To modify fields that show in the Query Builder:

1. Go to any of your Business Contact Manager views (Accounts, Business Contacts, Opportunities, etc.).
2. In the upper-right corner, locate the search bar. To the right of the search bar, you'll see a chevron (⊻). Click this icon to bring up the Query Builder.
3. Locate a field that is currently showing in the Query Builder that you do *not* want to use in your search. Click the field label for that field. (The field label is the text to the left of the field.)
4. A drop-down appears, and you can choose a new field to use in the Query Builder.

Need to include more fields in your search? Click the Add Criteria button in the lower-left corner of the Query Builder to add more field options for your search.

Applying filters

Filters in Business Contact Manager control what accounts, business contacts, opportunities, business projects, or other records appear in your views. Just about any view can have a filter applied.

Task A   Applying a simple filter

Applying a simple filter lets you quickly specify which records are displayed in your view. Just want to see all of your business contacts in Texas? Apply a filter, and all other contacts temporarily disappear.

Filters are not sticky. If you set a filter on a view, the filter is cleared as soon as you exit the program and re-open Business Contact Manager.

To apply a simple filter for a view:

1. Go to any of your Business Contact Manager views (Accounts, Business Contacts, Opportunities, etc.).
2. Right-click somewhere in the view and choose the Filter option.
3. In the Contacts tab, type a search term in the field.
4. In the drop-down, select the areas of the database where you'd like to search for the search term.
5. Click OK. Until you clear the filter or exit the program, this view will only show items that match your filter.

Task B Applying an advanced filter

If you want to display only business contacts, accounts, opportunities, or other database items that are in a certain category or that match a specified advanced query, you can set an advanced filter on the view.

To apply an advanced filter for a view:

1. Go to any of your Business Contact Manager views (Accounts, Business Contacts, Opportunities, etc.).
2. Right-click somewhere in the view and choose the Filter option.
3. In the More Choices tab, you can choose to filter by category, flagged status, and more.
4. In the Advanced tab, you can specify an advanced query.
5. Click OK. Until you clear the filter or exit the program, this view will only show items that match your filter.

If you are a SQL expert, you can write a SQL statement in the SQL tab to create an advanced filter.

You can only add 20 conditions to a filter.

Working with Search Folders

Search folders are virtual folders that let you display data based on a pre-defined filter. You could have a Search Folder that shows all new contacts created in the last 30 days. You might have another Search Folder that shows opportunities that are set to close this week. If there is a subset of your database that you want to repeatedly reference, create a Search Folder.

Task A   Creating a Search Folder

You can create an unlimited number of Search Folders, and Search Folders for Business Contact Manager are separate from e-mail Search Folders you might have created in Outlook. Once you have a Search Folder created, you can create a marketing campaign from the Search Folder, or you could show the Search Folder in your Business Contact Manager Home screen.

Types of Search Folders:
- Business Contacts
- Accounts
- Opportunities
- Business Projects
- Project Tasks
- Business Contact History
- Account History
- Opportunity History
- Business Project History

To create a Search Folder for business contacts:

1. Click the Business Contact Manager Home button on the toolbar.
2. On the left panel, you'll see a folder called Search Folders. Within that folder, you'll see a list of all of your existing Search Folders, if there are any.
3. Right-click the Search Folders folder and select the New Search Folder option.
4. Give your Search Folder a name.
5. From the drop-down, select the type of database items that should be included in the Search Folder. (A list of types is listed in the sidebar on this page.)
6. Click the Filter button to specify a filter for this Search Folder.
7. Click OK to save your changes.

Task B   Modifying an existing Search Folder

Anyone who has access to your Search Folder will be able to modify attributes for the Search Folder.

To modify the filter set for an existing Search Folder:

1. Right-click the Search Folder you'd like to modify.
2. Choose the Customize this Search Folder option.
3. Change any attributes. See the previous task for more information on Search Folder attributes.
4. Click OK.

Right-click a Search Folder and choose the Delete *"Name of Folder"* option to delete the Search Folder. Deleting a Search Folder only deletes the folder; it doesn't delete any of the items contained in the folder.

Task C   Adding a Search Folder to the Business Contact Manager Home screen

If you want to be able to easily access a Search Folder, you can add a shortcut to the Search Folder from the Business Contact Manager Home screen. There are four pages on the Home screen: Home, Sales, Marketing, and Projects. You can add a Search Folder to any of these pages.

To add a Search Folder to the Business Contact Manager Home screen:

1. Click the Business Contact Manager Home button to get to the Business Contact Manager Home screen.
2. Go to the page where you'd like to add the shortcut.
3. Click Add or Remove Content.
4. Select your Search Folder from the list.
5. Click Move Up or Move Down to change the position of the Search Folder on the Home screen.
6. Click OK to save your changes.

Once you've added a Search Folder to the Business Contact Manager Home screen, you can right-click in the Search Folder on the Home screen and select the Field Choose option to customize the fields that display for contacts in the Search Folder.

Chapter 6

Managing Your Calendar and Tasks

- Viewing and navigating the calendar
- Linking appointments with business contacts and opportunities
- Adding appointment details
- Categorizing activities
- Finding activities
- Working with tasks

Viewing and navigating the calendar

Outlook is the most popular calendar program in the world. Chances are good that you're already using it to manage your day-to-day appointments. While this book does cover some calendaring functions within Outlook, we focus on the Outlook Business Contact Manager calendar integration.

Task A   Viewing and printing the calendar

Outlook 2007 does a good job of helping you manage your calendar and follow up tasks. When you combine the Outlook calendar with the powerful contact management functionality of Business Contact Manager, you can then easily manage all of your appointments, meetings, events, tasks, and project tasks, and associate those activities with accounts, business contacts, or opportunities.

If you've been an Outlook Calendar user for any length of time, you will be right at home in these views. And with the added functionality of linking calendar items to Business Contact Manager accounts, business contacts, or opportunities, you will be able to better view, track, and manage all of your activities.

To view your day, week, or month calendars:

1. Click Go | Calendar, or click Calendar in the Outlook 2007 Navigation Pane.
2. Click a date in the Calendar Navigator that appears in the Calendar Navigation Pane. You will be taken to the daily view of the calendar in Outlook 2007.
3. You can use the buttons at the top to view a day, week, or month view of the calendar. You can also use the forward and back buttons to the left of the date to move around the calendar by day, week, or month, depending on the view.
4. Click on the Week view button. Notice the radio buttons next to the Calendar view buttons. These let you toggle between the workweek view, Monday through Friday, and the view of an entire week, including the weekend days.
5. Now click on the Month view button. The radio buttons let you select the level of detail to show.
6. Use the mini calendar in the Navigation Pane to view future dates in any view, day, week, or month. To get back to the current day, click Go | Today.

Task B   Viewing details for an appointment on the calendar

When viewing the calendar in the day, week, or month view, you will be able to see your appointments, meetings, events, and tasks easily, but you can include quite a bit of additional detailed information when you create an activity, so viewing those additional details is quite useful.

To view details for an appointment on the calendar:

1. Click Go | Calendar, or click Calendar in the Outlook 2007 Navigation Pane.
2. Navigate to the day on the calendar for an appointment you would like to view.
3. You can either double-click on the appointment to open it or right-click and select Open.
4. You will now be able to view the details of the appointment.

When you are viewing the details for an appointment, you can also make changes to that appointment and when you click Save & Close those changes will be saved.

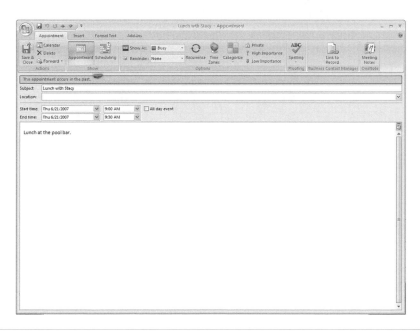

Task C   Using the To-Do Bar to navigate

The To-Do Bar contains a mini calendar that you can use to navigate the calendar quickly. If you can master the nuances of this mini calendar, then you will be able to easily maneuver through your calendar.

To use the To-Do Bar's mini calendar to navigate:

1. Click Go | Calendar, or click Calendar in the Outlook 2007 Navigation Pane.
2. Click View | To-Do Bar | Normal to toggle the To-Do Bar. You want to make sure the To-Do Bar is displayed. The mini calendar shows at the top of the To-Do Bar.
3. You can click on any day in the mini calendar to quickly go to that day.
4. You can click on the arrow keys on either side of the name of the month in the mini calendar to skip forward or backward a month.
5. If you click and hold the left mouse button while on the name of the month in the mini calendar, a list of six months pops up. You can quickly switch to a different month by selecting that month from the list.
6. If you start in the daily view, you can click and drag your mouse over a week to bring up that week in the Week view.
7. In the day or week view of the calendar, you can click on the days of the week in the mini calendar to display the month view.
8. In the day, week, or month view of the calendar, you can click and drag over any number of days, and you will then be viewing those days on your calendar.

If you are on a day in the calendar with no appointment details, you will see two vertical blue tabs appear on either side of that day, week, or month. The tab on the left will take you to the most recent previous appointment on the calendar, and the tab on the right will take you to your next scheduled appointment.

Task D   Printing your calendar

Having your calendar stored electronically in Outlook is great, and you can certainly synchronize your Outlook calendar easily with most PDA (Personal Digital Assistant) devices. But sometimes you just need a good old-fashioned paper calendar. Or perhaps you want to provide a copy of your calendar to other folks in your organization who cannot view your calendar directly. In either case, having a paper version of your calendar can be useful.

To print your calendar:

1. Click Go | Calendar, or click Calendar in the Outlook 2007 Navigation Pane.
2. Select a day, week, or month view of the calendar.
3. Click File | Print.
4. Select a printer.
5. In the Print style section, Outlook automatically selects the style corresponding to the view you were in, so if you were in the week view, the Weekly style will be selected. If you want to print a different view or style, simply select that style from the list.
6. In the Print range section, you can select the start and end dates and if you want to hide the details of private appointments on the printed calendar.
7. Click the Preview button in the lower-left corner to see how the calendar will look when printed. If the preview looks acceptable, click Print or Close and then click OK.

You can print a blank calendar in Outlook 2007 as well. Click File | New | Folder. Give this new folder a name, like Company Vacation & Holiday calendar. In the Folder contains drop-down, click Calendar items. In the Select where to place the folder area, click Calendar, then click OK. Back in the calendar view in Outlook, in the Navigation Pane, the new calendar will appear under the My Calendars section. You can open this new, blank calendar and then print.

Linking appointments with business contacts and opportunities

Managing activities associated with accounts, business contacts, opportunities, or business projects is an important function of Business Contact Manager. You can create an appointment from the Business Contact Manager record so that it will be linked to that Business Contact Manager record. For example, if you create an appointment to meet with a business contact, then that appointment will be linked to that business contact.

Task A Scheduling an appointment with an existing contact or opportunity

You can schedule an appointment with a business contact in a couple of ways. You can go to the business contact first, and then create the new appointment, but for many people, scheduling is more easily done by viewing your calendar to see available times. In that case you can create the appointment on the Outlook 2007 Calendar directly and simply link it to the appropriate Business Contact or Account.

To create a new appointment from a business contact:

1. Go to your list of business contacts. You can get there by clicking Business Contact Manager | Business Contacts.
2. Select the business contact by clicking once on the contact.
3. Click Actions | Create | New Appointment with Business Contact.
4. Enter the Subject of the appointment, and then use the tab key to move your cursor to the Location and enter where the appointment will take place.
5. Now click in the Start time drop-down and select the date of the appointment from the Calendar drop-down. Click the Time drop-down and select the Start time. Then click in the End time drop-down and select the end time for the appointment.

You can also use the handy right-click functionality to create a new appointment with a business contact. Simply right-click on a business contact, then select Create | New Appointment with Business Contact and follow the rest of the instructions to schedule the appointment.

6. Click in the large white area and enter any details about the appointment, such as the agenda or information about the location.
7. Click the Save & Close button.

Task B	Linking an existing calendar item to a business contact, account, opportunity, or business project

Scheduling things directly on the calendar is quick and easy, but those meetings or appointments won't be automatically linked to any of the entities in your Business Contact Manager database. Since part of the powerful functionality of a contact management system is the ability to see all of the associated history and activities for a contact, you'll want to link your calendar items to the appropriate business contact entity.

To link an existing calendar item to a business contact:

1. On the calendar, double-click an appointment or meeting to open. (For this example, you will link an appointment on the calendar to a business contact, but the steps are the same to link a meeting or appointment to an account, opportunity, or business project.)

2. In the Business Contact group of the ribbon, click the Link to Record button.

3. This will open the Link to Business Contact Manager record dialog box. In the Folder drop-down, select Business Contacts. A list of your business contacts appears. You can either search for a name in the Search box by typing the first and last name of the business contact or click on a name in the list.

4. Click the Link To button to add that business contact to the linked Records box and click OK. Or you can double-click the business contact name, which will populate the Link to box, then click OK.

5. Note here that you can link this calendar item to multiple Business Contact Manager entities, not just to business contacts. You can link a meeting or appointment with an account, an opportunity, and a business project.

6. Now click Save & Close.

When you are linking to a Business Contact Manager entity like a business contact, you can also create a new business contact on the fly. Just click the New button and add the information on the new business contact. Or you can add more information to an existing contact by clicking Open.

One glaring omission of the integration between the Outlook 2007 calendar and Business Contact Manager is the inability to view your calendar and see what activities are linked to Business Contact Manager. Because this is not possible, you might want to put the account name, business contact name, opportunity title, or business project name in the Subject line of the activity.

Task C Scheduling events

Events are activities that occur on a specific date but do not take up a specific block of time on your calendar. They are useful for scheduling things like conferences, trade shows, and vacations. They are also well-suited to things like birthdays, anniversaries, and holidays. Events are shown on the calendar as banners at the top of day, or across multiple days if the event goes on longer than one day.

To create a new event:

1. For this task, we will use the monthly view of the calendar. Go to your month calendar.
2. Click Actions | New All Day Event.
3. Enter all of the details for your event and click the Save & Close button.
4. You now have an event on your calendar, but it's not linked to any business contact, account opportunity, or business project.
5. To link an event to a business contact, account, opportunity, or business project, double-click to open the event and then link it to a Business Contact Manager entity, just like we did in the previous Task B in this chapter. Or, you can simply right-click the event on the calendar, and select Link to Record. Then you can select the folder to choose accounts, business contacts, opportunities, or business projects, double-click the entity to populate the Link to box, and click OK.

You can have Outlook add standard holidays to your calendar. Click Tools | Options and then select Calendar Options. In the Calendar options section, click the Add Holidays button. Click the check box in front of your country to select that country. You can also add more than one country's holidays to your calendar, in case you need to know that May 1 is Labor Day in Italy. Click OK twice and you will now be able to view the holidays, which appear as all-day events on your calendar.

Task D Unlinking a calendar entry

You might want to unlink a calendar entry from a particular Business Contact Manager entity but still leave that activity on the calendar. This task will show you how to do that from the calendar entry itself. The next task will walk you through the steps to delete the calendar item from the Communication History section in Business Contact Manager.

When you *delete* a calendar item (appointment, meeting, event, or to-do) from the Communication History view of a business contact, account, opportunity, or business project, it *does not* delete that appointment from the calendar. Deleting an item in the Communication History view on a business contact simply unlinks that calendar entry from the Business Contact Manager entity. So, in this case, *delete* really means *unlink*.

To unlink a calendar item from a business contact:

1. Double-click the calendar item you want to unlink. (For this example, we will be unlinking an appointment from a business contact, but the steps are the same to unlink a meeting or appointment from an account, opportunity, or business project.)
2. In the Business Contact Manager group on the ribbon, click the Link to Record button.
3. This will open the Link to Business Contact Manager Record dialog box.
4. In the Link To box, highlight the business contact name and press the Delete key on your keyboard. Click OK and then click Save & Close.

Adding appointment details

Getting an activity on the calendar for a specific date and time is a great first step, but you can add so much more information in the activity details. You can add a reminder, schedule a recurring activity, manage meetings in different time zones, send meeting invitations via e-mail to participants, attach a file, and assign a category to that activity.

Task A   Setting reminders

When you schedule an activity in Outlook, you can set a reminder for that activity so that you will be prompted about an upcoming appointment, meeting, event, or task. You can set a reminder to electronically nudge you anywhere from five minutes before the activity up to two weeks before the activity.

To set a reminder:

1. Click Go | Calendar, or click Calendar in the Outlook 2007 Navigation Pane.
2. Select an appointment you have scheduled on your calendar, right-click, and select Open.
3. On the Appointment tab, in the Options group on the ribbon, select the drop-down next to the reminder icon, which looks like a small gold bell.
4. Select the amount of time prior to the appointment that you would like the reminder to appear.
5. Click Save & Close.

Reminders are basically electronic nagging; Outlook will gently remind you when you have important tasks or meetings coming up. As a former abuser of alarms, let me offer one piece of advice. If you set alarms for absolutely everything, then they tend to lose their effectiveness and you spend way too much time snoozing them.

The default reminder options available in the reminder pull-down are just a start. You can manually type in any reminder timeframe. Need to be reminded to do something nine days before a task? Just type "9 days" in the reminder box, then click Save & Close. Nine days before the task, Outlook will dutifully pop up that reminder.

Task B   Scheduling a recurring appointment

Some activities have to be done every day, week, or month, in which case you can easily set up and manage recurring activities in Outlook. Common examples of recurring activities include submitting your sales forecast weekly, the ever-popular regular staff meeting, or submitting your expenses monthly.

To schedule a recurring appointment:

1. Go to the Outlook calendar view. Click Go | Calendar or click on Calendar in the Outlook Navigation Pane.
2. Click on the day you want to schedule the appointment in the mini calendars on the left.
3. Double-click on the start time for the recurring appointment. Enter the subject, location, and start/end dates and times for the appointment.
4. On the Appointment tab on the ribbon, in the Options group, click on Recurrence.
5. In the Recurrence pattern section, select Daily, Weekly, Monthly, or Yearly and indicate the appropriate recurrence settings for the selection.
6. In the Range of recurrence section, you can set the end date, selecting either no end date, end after a specific number of occurrences, or end by a specific date.
7. Click OK | Save & Close.

One of the best uses of recurring activities is to set up recurring annual events for birthdays and anniversaries. You can schedule important birthdays and anniversaries as recurring events with a reminder a week (or more) before the event. Acting on the reminder is still up to you, but at least Outlook is doing its part.

Task C Inviting others to participate in your meeting

You can schedule a meeting with your Business Contact Manager business contacts and then send a meeting invitation via e-mail to all the invited participants. Outlook will then track the responses from the participants, allowing you to more easily plan and manage meetings.

To invite others to participate in your meeting:

1. Go to your list of business contacts. You can get there by clicking Business Contact Manager | Business Contacts.
2. Select the business contact by clicking once on the contact.
3. Click Actions | Create | New Meeting Request to Business Contact.
4. Enter the subject of the meeting and the location.
5. Select the date, start, and end times.
6. Click in the large white area and enter any details about the appointment, such as the agenda or information about the location.
7. Click the Send button to send the meeting invitation to your business contact.

When your business contact receives the meeting invitation, he has the option to accept, tentatively accept, decline, or propose a new time. When he accepts, it will add that meeting to his Outlook calendar, if he uses Outlook—even if he uses an older version of Outlook. To track who has responded to your meeting invitation, open the meeting on your calendar, then in the Show group on the ribbon select Tracking. This will display the responses that have been received to date.

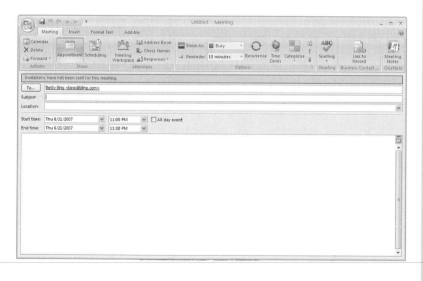

Task D   Attaching files to a meeting request

You may need to provide material to meeting attendees prior to a meeting. With Business Contact Manager, you can create the meeting request and attach files to the invitation e-mail so that all participants will have any files needed prior to the meeting. And those file attachments will be a part of the business contact's communication history so that you can easily refer back to the materials that you sent for a meeting, right from the business contact's record in the database.

To attach a file to a meeting request:

1. Go to your list of business contacts. You can get there by clicking Business Contact Manager | Business Contacts.
2. Select the business contact by clicking once on the contact.
3. Click Actions | Create | New Meeting Request to Business Contact.
4. Enter the subject of the meeting and the location.
5. Select the date, start, and end times.
6. On the ribbon, click on the Insert tab and then in the Include group, select Attach File. Browse to the location on your computer where you want to select the file attachment, such as your Documents, select the file, and click the Insert button. Your attached file will now show in the details area of the meeting request.
7. Click Send. Now, go back to that business contact's record, and in the Show group on the ribbon, click History. You will see the meeting invitation you sent via e-mail and the file will be attached to that e-mail message.

The History view of a business contact in Business Contact Manager is a bit of a misnomer. This view will also show you all the future scheduled appointments and meetings with that business contact, in the Chronological view.

Task E   Rescheduling activities

"The only thing constant in life is change." Francois de la Rochefoucauld, (1613-1680). Nowhere is that more true, it seems, than with your schedule. Luckily, rescheduling an activity in Outlook is relatively easy and painless.

To reschedule an activity:

1. Click Go | Calendar, or click Calendar in the Outlook 2007 Navigation Pane.
2. Select an appointment you need to reschedule on your calendar, right-click, and select Open.
3. Make any changes to the appointment, including changing the new start/end dates and times.
4. Click Save & Close.
5. Or, you can drag and drop the appointment to the new date and time on the calendar. Click on the appointment and while holding down the left mouse button, drag that appointment to the new date/time.

If you are in the day or week view of the calendar, and you are viewing an appointment you need to move to later in the month, you can click on the appointment (holding down the left mouse button) and drag that appointment to a date later in the month on the mini calendar on the right side of the calendar view. This will move the appointment to the same time, but on a new day, and will take you to the new day's view on the calendar where you can adjust the time, if necessary.

In the Advanced options area of the Calendar options, you can tell Outlook how to process meeting requests that you receive from others. This is helpful if you are responsible for coordinating resources, like conference rooms. In the Calendar options, under the Advanced options section, click resource scheduling and select your default settings.

Task F   Setting calendar preferences

You can set up some basic calendar preferences in Outlook, which will make scheduling activities much faster. You can configure the calendar options to show specific information and to manage things like your default responses to meeting requests.

To set calendar preferences:

1. Click Tools | Options and on the Preferences tab, in the Calendar section, you can select the default reminder time by clicking in the Reminder drop-down.

2. For more calendar preference settings, click the Calendar Options button.

3. In the Calendar workweek section, you can select the days of the week to be included in the workweek view, the first day of the week, the first week of the year, and start time and end times for the calendar.

4. In the Calendar options section, you can set preferences for the view and behavior of the calendar.

5. In the Advanced options section you can set more preferences for things like defining your default free/busy options, resource scheduling, and time zone.

6. Click OK twice.

Categorizing activities

You can categorize just about anything in Business Contact Manager, and activities are no exception. Categorizing activities distinguishes them visually on the calendar, and you can set a filter in the All Calendar Items view to only show activities in a certain category.

Task A   Categorizing an appointment

The categorization feature of Business Contact Manager lets you group accounts, business contacts, opportunities, business projects, and project tasks together by assigning a category. This same feature applies to activities such as meetings, appointments, events, and tasks. Most of the views in Outlook and Business Contact Manager offer the option of seeing all of your information by category. You can view your calendar or task list by category so that you can more easily manage related activities.

To categorize an appointment:

1. Click Go | Calendar, or click Calendar in the Outlook 2007 Navigation Pane.
2. Select an appointment you would like to categorize, right-click, and select Open.
3. On the Appointment tab on the ribbon, in the Options group, click Categorize.
4. Select the category from the drop-down menu.
5. Click Save & Close.

Categorization is a very useful and powerful function of Business Contact Manager; we cover categories in detail in Chapter 4.

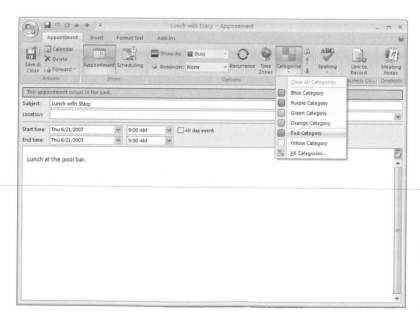

Viewing your calendar items by category is a useful function. For example, you may want to categorize all your client meetings and when you view your calendar by category, all of the client meetings will be grouped together, and Outlook will provide a count of the total client meetings as well.

Task B   Viewing appointments by category

You can easily view all of your appointments, meetings, and events by category. If you create a category for clients, for example, then you can quickly view all of the calendar items that are associated with clients when you view the calendar by category.

To view appointments by a category:

1. Click Go | Calendar, or click Calendar in the Outlook 2007 Navigation Pane.
2. Click View | Current View | By Category.
3. You will now be viewing your appointments, meetings, and events by category.
4. To return to the basic calendar view, click View | Current View | Day/Week/Month.

Finding activities

In Outlook 2007 with Business Contact Manager, you can view your activities in a number of different ways and you can quickly search the calendar for a particular word or phrase. You can also view other user's calendars, provided you are in an Exchange environment and that user has granted you permission to view her calendar.

Task A Viewing activities scheduled with a business contact or opportunity

The core of any contact management system is the ability to quickly and easily see a snapshot of the interaction with a particular contact. Business Contact Manager provides that on accounts, business contacts, and opportunities through the History view.

To view activities scheduled with a business contact or opportunity:

1. Go to your list of business contacts. You can get there by clicking Business Contact Manager | Business Contacts.
2. Double-click on a business contact.
3. In the Show group on the ribbon, click History
4. You will see a list of all the communication history items for that business contact.
5. On the View drop-down at the top of the screen, select Chronological.
6. You will now see all the communication history items, including appointments, grouped by date.
7. Click Save & Close.

When you view the history for an account, a business contact, or an opportunity, it's not strictly history. You will see all of the activities, both those in the past and the activities scheduled for the future. When perusing the History view, it's helpful to select the Chronological view option so that you can easily see the true history that has already occurred, as differentiated from the activities that have not yet occurred.

The Search function is an easy way to group related calendar items together. For example, if you noted in the details of your meetings a specific agenda item such as "Proposal Review," you can search all your calendar items to find the appointments and meetings that all share that same agenda item.

Task B   Searching the calendar

You can search your calendar to find key words, phrases, or names. If you want to see all the calendar items for a particular business contact, you can search for that person's name on the calendar and then view all of the activities associated with that business contact.

To search the calendar:

1. Click Go | Calendar, or click Calendar in the Outlook 2007 Navigation Pane. You will see a Search Calendar box in the top-right corner of the calendar view.
2. Click in the Search Calendar box and enter your search word(s), phrase(s), or the name of a business contact.
3. As you type, Outlook will display the search results for the activities that match the search term(s).
4. To return to the regular calendar view, click the x next to the Search Calendar box where your search term(s) are showing.

Task C   Viewing other user's calendars

You can create and track multiple calendars in Outlook 2007. Or, if you're using Microsoft Exchange, you can set up Outlook to view another user's calendar. This example assumes that you are using Exchange and that the other user has granted you permission to view his calendar.

To view another users' calendar:

1. On the left-hand side of the Outlook Navigation Pane, select Calendar and click Open a Shared Calendar.
2. Type the name of the other user or click to select a name from the address book and click OK.
3. The other user's calendar appears next to yours.
4. Now that you have viewed another user's calendar, his calendar is added to the Navigation Pane so that you can simply click on that calendar in the Navigation Pane to open it.

Once you have set up the other user's calendar, you can quickly go to the view of his calendar by clicking on the user's calendar in the My Calendars section on the left-hand side of the Outlook Navigation Pane. If you select the check box in front of two or more calendars in that section, Outlook will display the calendars side by side so that you can view multiple calendars at once.

Working with tasks

Managing your list of to-do's can sometimes be overwhelming. Outlook with Business Contact Manager makes creating, tracking, delegating, and viewing your tasks a much less daunting task. If you find yourself making paper lists of things to do, or if your computer monitor is ringed by cryptic notes on Post-Its, consider managing those important tasks in Business Contact Manager instead.

Task A   Creating a task linked to a business contact

Managing tasks associated with accounts, business contacts, opportunities, or business projects is an important function of Business Contact Manager. You can create a task from the Business Contact Manager record so that it will be linked to that Business Contact Manager record. For example, if you create a task to call a prospect from that prospect's Business Contact Manager record, then that task will be linked to that business contact.

To create a task linked to a business contact:

1. Go to your list of business contacts. You can get there by clicking Business Contact Manager | Business Contacts. (For this example, you will create a task from a business contact, but the steps are the same to create and link a task to an account, opportunity, or business project.)
2. Select the business contact by clicking once on the contact.
3. Click Actions | Create | New Task for Business Contact.
4. Enter the subject of the task, the start and due dates, status, priority, and percentage complete.
5. Click in the large white area and enter any details about the task.
6. Click the Save & Close button.

You can link tasks with the following Business Contact Manager record types:

- Accounts
- Business Contacts
- Opportunities
- Business Projects

Task B   Creating a task not linked with anyone in the database

Managing tasks associated with accounts, business contacts, opportunities, or business projects is an important function of Business Contact Manager, but most people need to manage tasks that are not related to an account or business contact record. Many tasks are just things you need to get done in your life or job, and are more general in nature. In Task A, we created a task from the Business Contact Manager record, which automatically linked the task to the Business Contact Manager record. Now we'll review how to create a non-linked task.

To create a task not linked with anyone in the database:

1. Click Go | Calendar and then Go | Tasks.
2. Click Actions | New Task.
3. Enter the subject of the task, the start and due dates, status, priority, and percentage complete.
4. Click in the large white area and enter any details about the task.
5. Click the Save & Close button.

If you have created a task in Outlook, you can still link that task to a Business Contact Manager record. For example, let's say you create a task to call a prospect, but that prospect has not been entered in your Business Contact Manager list of business contacts. Once you create the business contact in Business Contact Manager, you can open that task and link it to that business contact record in Business Contact Manager.

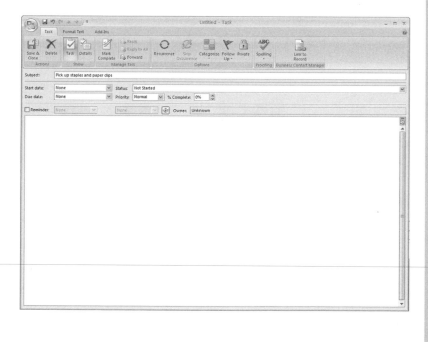

Task C   Creating a recurring task

Some tasks provide the singular joy of needing to be done over and over—like submitting expense reports or pipeline reports to your manager. You can easily create recurring tasks to help you manage those tasks more efficiently.

To create a recurring task:

1. Click Go | Tasks or click on Tasks in the Outlook Navigation Pane.
2. Click Actions | New Task.
3. Enter the subject of the task, start and due dates, status, priority, and percentage complete.
4. Click in the large white area and enter any details about the task.
5. In the Options group on the ribbon, click on Recurrence.
6. In the Recurrence pattern section, select Daily, Weekly, Monthly, or Yearly and indicate the appropriate recurrence settings for the selection.
7. In the Range of recurrence section, you can set the end date, selecting either no end date, end after a specific number of occurrences, or end by a specific date.
8. Click OK | Save & Close.

If you need to do a particular task on a regular basis, setting that task up as a recurring task allows you to create one task that will repeat daily, weekly, monthly, or annually, as long as you need it to recur.

Task D Editing a task

Sometimes completing a particular task involves a single swift and decisive action. Some tasks, on the other hand, require work over time, in bits and pieces, and may even require you to wait for input from other people. You can edit an existing task to update the status, percentage complete, or priority. Or maybe you need to push out the due date of a task. You can easily open and edit an existing task so that the information on the task reflects the most up-to-date information.

To edit a task:

1. Click Go | Tasks or click on Tasks in the Outlook Navigation pane.
2. Select the task you want to edit from the list and right-click and select Open.
3. Make any changes to the task, including changing the new start or due dates, the status, priority, and percentage complete.
4. Click Save & Close.

If your task list is overwhelming, try viewing only those tasks due in the next seven days. Just click the radio button in front of Next Seven Days in the Current view section of the Navigation Pane in your task list view.

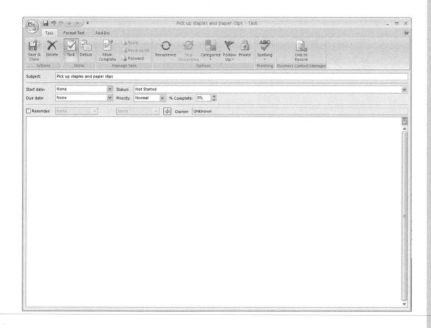

Task E   Deleting a task

You can edit a task or mark it complete, but sometimes you just need to delete it. When you delete a task, it is removed from your task list.

When you delete a task, it is really deleted. Unlike e-mail messages, accounts, business contact, and opportunities, tasks cannot be recovered from the Deleted Items folder in the Outlook Navigation Pane.

To delete a task:

1. Click Go | Tasks or click on Tasks in the Outlook Navigation Pane.
2. Select the task you want to edit from the list and right-click and select Delete.

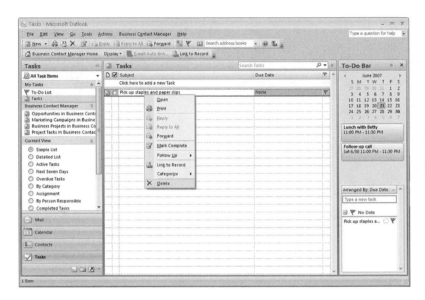

Task F   Assigning a task to another user

Delegating a task to another user in Business Contact Manager is easy. Making sure that they actually complete the task is another matter, and it is not covered in the subject matter in this book. Assigning a task to another user is a very straightforward process.

To assign a task to another user:

1. Click Go | Tasks or click on Tasks in the Outlook Navigation Pane.
2. Select the task you want to assign to another user from the list, right-click and select Open.
3. In the Manage Task group on the ribbon, click Assign Task.
4. Type the user's name in the To box and click Send.
5. The task will be sent to the user via e-mail.

When you assign a task to another user, that user will receive an e-mail with the task. If she accepts the task, then that task is added to her task list.

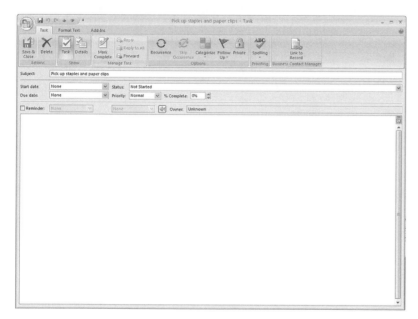

Task G   Marking a task as complete

Completing a task might take considerable effort, but marking that task as complete in Business Contact Manager is quick and easy.

To mark a task as complete:

1. Click Go | Tasks or click on Tasks in the Outlook Navigation Pane.
2. Click the check box next to the task you want to clear.
3. That task now appears on your list with a line through it, indicating that the task is complete.
4. If you open the completed task, you will see that Outlook updated the Status to Complete and the percentage complete to 100%.

When you complete a task, you can actually send a status report via e-mail about that task. Simply open the task and in the Manage Task group on the ribbon, click Send Status Report. You can then select the contact or business contact to whom to send the report, and click Send.

Task H Looking at your tasks in the task views

Tasks can be viewed in three locations: the To-Do Bar, in Tasks on the Outlook Navigation Pane, and in the Daily task list in the calendar.

To look at your tasks in the task views:

1. Click Go | Tasks or click on Tasks in the Outlook Navigation Pane.
2. You will be in the Task or To-Do List view.
3. In the Navigation Pane, there are several View options, such as a simple list, a detailed list, overdue tasks, and more.
4. To view the To-Do Bar, click View | To-Do Bar | Normal. The To-Do Bar will be displayed in a pane on the right side of your screen, with the mini calendar at the top and a list of your appointments and tasks below the mini calendar.
5. To view your tasks in your calendar, click on Calendar in the Outlook Navigation Pane. Then click View | Daily Task List | Normal. Now your tasks will appear in a pane at the bottom of your day or week calendar view.

To print your task list, simply open the task list view by clicking Task in the Outlook Navigation Pane, and then click File | Print.

Chapter 7

Opportunity Management

- Adding and removing opportunities
- Adding communication history items
- Viewing opportunities
- Managing products and services

Adding and removing opportunities

Tracking sales opportunities is one of the most powerful functions of Business Contact Manager. You can create and track an opportunity through the sales cycle, including all of the communication and interaction with a customer or prospect as it relates to a potential opportunity. Managing your opportunities and all the related tasks and history items in Business Contact Manager is a great way to gain visibility into your sales cycle, and a great tool to help sell more effectively.

Task A   Entering a new opportunity

Entering new opportunities in Business Contact Manager is simple and straightforward. When you enter an opportunity, you can add a number of details about that potential deal, including things like the expected close date, the probability or likelihood that you will win that opportunity, and more.

To enter a new opportunity:

1. Click Business Contact Manager | Opportunities. This takes you to the list view of all your opportunities.
2. Click Actions | New opportunity. This brings up the opportunity form.
3. Give this new opportunity a title.
4. To link this opportunity to a business contact or an account, click the Link To button and select Accounts or Business Contacts from the Folder drop-down. Select the business contact or account and click Link To and OK.
5. You can enter a lot of details about opportunities in the following sections: Source information, Status, Terms, and Product and services sections.
6. Click Save & Close.

> There is a lot of information that you can track for opportunities, most of which is optional. Opportunities are required to have two pieces of information though—a title and a linked account or business contact.

Task B Editing an existing opportunity

As you work on a potential opportunity, you will need to update that opportunity to move it through your sales process. You use the Edit function to update the opportunity as it moves through the sales cycle. The sales stage, expected close date, probability, and total expected revenue are probably the most common elements that change throughout the sales process, but when you are editing an opportunity, you can update any new or changed information that you uncover along the way.

To edit an existing opportunity:

1. Click Business Contact Manager | Opportunities. This takes you to the list view of all your opportunities.
2. Double-click the opportunity you want to edit.
3. Update the information for the opportunity, such as the Sales stage, Close date, or Probability.
4. Click Save & Close.

In the Source information area, you can track the business contact that originally initiated the opportunity, which might not be the same person that you have the opportunity linked to. When you click the Initiated By button, you will get a dialog box that lets you pick the business contact that initiated the opportunity.

Task C | Deleting an opportunity

Deleting an opportunity is as easy as adding a new opportunity. Anyone who can access your database can delete an opportunity. We cover sharing your database in Chapter 1. You should only delete opportunities that are no longer valid, but you wouldn't want to delete an opportunity that you lost. The next task reviews how to close an opportunity and track your sales wins and losses.

Whoops—you didn't mean to delete that opportunity. Don't panic, you can restore an opportunity from the Deleted Items folder. Instructions on restoring items from the Deleted Items folder appear in Chapter 2.

To delete an opportunity:

1. Click Business Contact Manager | Opportunities. This takes you to the list view of all your opportunities.
2. Double-click the opportunity you want to edit.
3. In the Actions group on the ribbon, click Delete.

Task D Closing an opportunity

The final stage in the sales process is closing, and the result is either a win or a loss. Tracking your wins and losses is a great tool to better understand how to be more successful in your sales efforts. In Business Contact Manager, when you close an opportunity, you can indicate the final outcome of that deal. Later in this chapter, we will cover how to customize the view of your sales opportunities, and one of the options is to view your opportunities by sales stage.

To close an opportunity:

1. Click Business Contact Manager | Opportunities. This takes you to the list view of all your opportunities.
2. Double-click the opportunity you want to close.
3. Click in the Sales stage drop-down in the Status area and select either Closed Won or Closed Lost.
4. Click Save & Close.

In Chapter 12 we review dashboards. You can create a section of your dashboard to show all Closed Won and Closed Lost opportunities.

Adding communication history items

Communication history items in Business Contact Manager include things like an appointment, a business note, an e-mail message, a file, or a task. Communication history items can be linked to accounts, business contacts, business projects, or opportunities. By linking communication history items with an opportunity, you can track all of the interaction and communication that are related to that opportunity. When you link an opportunity to a business contact, that opportunity will also appear as a communication history item on the business contact's record.

Task A   Adding a note for an opportunity

Once you have created an opportunity, you might find it helpful to add notes for that opportunity. You can add an unlimited number of business notes for a business contact, and each note can be as long as you need it to be. Business Notes in Business Contact Manager are a type of communication history item, and when you add a business note from an opportunity, that business note will automatically be linked to that opportunity.

To add a note for an opportunity:

1. Click Business Contact Manager | Opportunities. This takes you to the list view of all your opportunities.
2. Double-click the opportunity for which you want to create a note.
3. In the Communicate group on the ribbon, click New History Item | Business Note.
4. Enter the subject of the note and then click in the Comments section to write the note itself.
5. Click Save & Close.

You can add multiple business notes to an opportunity, or you can create a single business note and add to that note throughout the life of that opportunity.

If you are going to be adding to a business note on an opportunity, you can add a time stamp to each entry on the note so that you can track the dates/times you added information to that business note. Business Contact Manager will assign a create date to the entire note.

Task B   Recording a phone log for an opportunity

Phone logs are just one type of communication that you can use to keep a record of your phone calls with accounts or business contacts. You can also create a phone log for an opportunity, which will allow you to track the specifics of phone calls related to that opportunity. You can track the subject, type, date, duration, and details of all of your phone calls.

To record a phone log for an opportunity:

1. Click Business Contact Manager | Opportunities. This takes you to the list view of all of your opportunities.
2. Double-click the opportunity to open the opportunity form.
3. In the Communicate group on the ribbon, click New History Item | Phone Log.
4. Enter the subject of the phone log, the Call type, and Call time information.
5. Click in the Comments section to enter the notes from the call.
6. Click Save & Close.

How many phone calls do you receive in a given day? How many phone calls do you make a day? The phone is a powerful business communication device, and tracking the pertinent details of your phone interaction as they relate to a sales opportunity is a smart way to manage all of those important interactions.

Task C   Creating a task for an opportunity

Do you keep a list of things you need to do? Those are tasks, and you can create and track all of the tasks associated with a specific opportunity in Business Contact Manager. You might have five to six stages in your sales cycle, such as prospecting, qualification, needs analysis, proposal, and negotiation. These stages are generally not specific activities, because most opportunities will require many follow-up activities, or tasks, to move that opportunity through the sales process to closure.

You can create and link the following history items with an opportunity:

- Business Note
- Phone Log
- Task
- Appointment
- File

To create a task for an opportunity:

1. Click Business Contact Manager | Opportunities. This takes you to the list view of all of your opportunities.
2. Double-click the opportunity for which you want to create a task to open that opportunity.
3. In the Communicate group on the ribbon, click New History Item | Task.
4. Enter the subject of the task, the start and due dates, the status, priority, and percentage complete.
5. Set a Reminder for yourself if you like.
6. Click Save & Close.

Task D   Creating an appointment for an opportunity

Appointments, like tasks, are the incremental activities that help you move a sales opportunity through the sales cycle to the all-important close. When you create a new appointment from an opportunity, Business Contact Manager will automatically link that appointment to both the opportunity and the account or business contact that is linked to the opportunity itself.

To create an appointment for an opportunity:

1. Click Business Contact Manager | Opportunities. This takes you to the list view of all your opportunities.
2. Double-click the opportunity for which you want to create a new appointment to open that opportunity.
3. In the Communicate group on the ribbon, click New History Item | Appointment.
4. Enter the subject, location, start, and end times for the appointment.
5. Click Save & Close.

In Chapter 6, we cover managing your calendar, including creating appointments and meeting invitations. If you are linking appointments to your opportunities, you might want to review that chapter for more information on creating and managing appointments and meetings.

You can also employ the very handy right-click function to add any of the communication history items to an opportunity. Simply click Business Contact Manager | Opportunities, then right-click on the opportunity and click Create. Now you can select the item of your choice—New Appointment, New Task, New Business Note, New Phone Log, or New Linked File.

Task E   Attaching a file to an opportunity

Tracking a deal through the pipeline often involves many different pieces of critical information, such as presentations, proposals, contracts, quotes, pricing, product, and other information. You can link any type of electronic files to an opportunity so that you will have all the relevant details right at your fingertips.

To attach a file to an opportunity:

1. Click Business Contact Manager | Opportunities. This takes you to the list view of all your opportunities.
2. Double-click the opportunity to open the opportunity form.
3. In the Communicate group on the ribbon, click New History Item | File.
4. Browse to the location of the file, click on the file name to select it, and click Open.

Viewing opportunities

The opportunity list view in Business Contact Manager allows you to manage all of the opportunities in your Business Contact Manager database. This overall view can be filtered and grouped in any number of ways to help you manage all of the deals in the pipeline. Chapter 3 covers, in detail, navigating and customizing the views in Business Contact Manager, which also applies to the opportunity view.

Task A   Viewing a list of opportunities

Having an aggregate view of all opportunities is a great feature, but the real power comes with the customization and filtering options available in this view. There are several standard views that will help you manage your opportunities, and the filtering option lets you drill down even further, helping you focus on specific opportunities.

To view a list of opportunities:

1. Click Business Contact Manager | Opportunities.
2. This takes you to the list view of all your opportunities.
3. In the Outlook Navigation Pane, in the Current View section, you can change the view to another default view option, such as By Sales Stage.
4. You can also change the columns of data you see in a view. Click Customize Current View below the Current View section in the Navigation Pane and then select Fields to add or remove fields from the view, as well as change the order of the fields.
5. You can print this view by clicking File | Print. This will print your opportunity list with the customizations you have made to this view.
6. In the list view of your opportunities, you can sort the current view by any of the column headers at the top, either ascending or descending, simply by clicking on the column header.

Opportunity view options include:

- By Assigned To
- By Expected Revenue
- By Linked To
- By Sales Stage
- Calendar
- Created By
- Open Opportunities List
- Recently Modified
- Timeline (Closed Date)
- Timeline (Delivery Date)

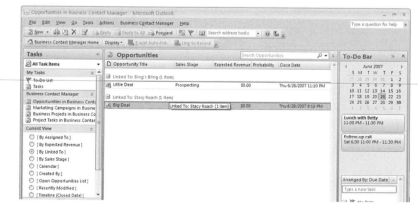

Task B Filtering the opportunity list view

The standard opportunity views are a good start on different ways to track and analyze your sales pipeline, but the filtering options in the opportunity list view offer even more powerful tools to help you with your opportunities. You can filter the opportunity list view by sales stage, close date, product, status, title, type, probability, assigned to user, total value, and more. Need to see all your deals in the negotiation stage that are closing this month and have a value of more than $5,000? The powerful filtering options will let you slice and dice your opportunity data in any number of ways.

To filter the opportunity list view:

1. Click Business Contact Manager | Opportunities. This takes you to the list view of all your opportunities, and you can select the view you would like to filter in the Current View area in the Outlook Navigation Pane.

2. Click Customize Current View below the Current View section in the Navigation Pane and click Filter or right-click anywhere in the white space on the opportunity list view and click Filter. This opens the Filter dialog box.

3. For this example, we will filter all of the opportunities that are due to close in the next seven days.

4. Click the Advanced tab.

5. Click Field | User Defined Fields in folder | Close Date.

6. In the Condition drop-down, select in the next 7 days and then click Add to List | OK.

7. You will now be viewing your opportunity list for all the deals that are due to close in the next seven days.

Task C   Removing filters from the opportunity list view

Filters, while very useful, are often the source of user consternation. When you apply a filter, you are only seeing the data that meets the filter criteria. Users will often apply a filter to the opportunity list view, and then go to another view in Business Contact Manager or Outlook, and when they return to the opportunity list view, they panic because they aren't seeing all of their opportunities. It's important to know how to remove those filters so that you can go back to the global view of your opportunities.

To remove a filter from the opportunity list view:

1. Click Business Contact Manager | Opportunities. This takes you to the list view of all your opportunities.
2. Right-click anywhere in the white space on the opportunity list view and click Filter. This opens the Filter dialog box.
3. Click the Advanced tab.
4. Highlight the filter item that you want to remove and click the Remove button.
5. Click OK. You will now be viewing all of your opportunities, without a filter applied.

In the Opportunity list view, any filters you create and apply to the view should be sticky, meaning that even when you close Business Contact Manager and re-open the application, the last filter you applied to your Opportunity view will still be applied to the list view. You'll know there is a filter applied because at the top of the Opportunity list, next to the search box, you will see the words (Filter Applied).

Notice that the term, "Communication History Item" is not quite accurate, because although the word "history" implies things in the past, in Business Contact Manager, communication history items also includes scheduled tasks, meetings, and appointments that have yet to occur.

Task D   Viewing communication items associated with an opportunity

Communication history items in Business Contact Manager include things like an appointment, a phone log, a business note, an e-mail message, a file, or a task. Communication history items can be linked to accounts, business contacts, business projects, or opportunities. By linking communication history items with an opportunity, you can track the interaction and communication that is related to that opportunity. Viewing the communication history items for an opportunity provides an overview of all of the interaction related to that opportunity.

To view communication items associated with an opportunity:

1. Click Business Contact Manager | Opportunities. This takes you to the list view of all your opportunities.
2. Double-click the opportunity for which you want to view the communication history items to open that opportunity.
3. In the Show group on the ribbon, click History.
4. You are now viewing all of the communication history items associated with that opportunity.

Managing products and services

In Business Contact Manager you can maintain a list of the products and/or services that your company sells. Along with the name of the product/service, you can also store a description of the item, as well as your unit cost for an item and the price for which you will sell that item.

Task A   Adding a new product or service

As you add product and/or service items to your Business Contact Manager database, they will be available when creating opportunities so that you can quickly pick the products or services that you are selling to a customer or prospect from this master list.

To add a new product or service:

1. Click Business Contact Manager | Product and Service Items List.
2. Click Add.
3. Enter the Item Name and Unit Price. Both of these items are required fields in the Add Product or Service dialog box.
4. You can also enter the following information about your product/service: Description, Default Quantity, Unit cost, Markup, and Unit Price, and if the product/service is taxable.
5. If you have more items to add, click the Add Next button, and continue entering products and/or services.
6. When you are finished entering your products or services, click Save and OK.

The currency used in your opportunities is set by your computer's regional settings. You cannot track multiple currencies in your opportunities in Business Contact Manager. To change the regional setting of your Windows XP computer, click Start | Control Panel | Regional and Language Options and then change the format to the correct country/region. For Vista, click Start | Control Panel | Clock, Language, and Region and then click Change the date, time, or number format and select your format.

Task B	**Deleting a product or service item**

One constant of life and business is change. You will likely change the products and services that your company sells over time. When you are no longer offering a particular product or service, you can remove that item from your master product and service list so that it is not available to select when creating new opportunities.

Unlike deleting other types of Business Contact Manager items, like contacts and opportunities, you cannot recover deleted product and service items from the Deleted Items folder in Business Contact Manager. Be very careful when deleting products and services.

To delete a product or service item:

1. Click Business Contact Manager | Product and Service Items List.
2. Click on the item you want to delete and click Delete.
3. Click Yes to confirm the deletion.
4. Click OK.

Task C   Importing a list of product or service items

You may already have a list of the products and services that your company sells, perhaps in an Excel spreadsheet. Business Contact Manager has a method for importing an existing list of products and services, making it easy to populate your master products and services list of items. You will probably need to do some formatting of that list because Business Contact Manager is fairly particular about the list format. Luckily there is good documentation of the required format available from the Help function on the Import wizard.

To import a list of product or service items:

1. Click Business Contact Manager | Product and Service Items List.
2. Click the Import button.
3. Click Browse to find the Comma Separated Values (.csv) format file.
4. In the Options area, choose the radio button in front of Add the items in this file to the existing list or, if you want to replace your existing product/service items with the information from your .csv file, select Replace existing list with items in this file. Note: this Replace option will replace your entire existing list of products and/or services.
5. The format of the data in the .csv file is critical, so be sure to click the Help button and view the Format your list of product and service items section.
6. Click Import. If there are errors with the import, you can click the View Log button to get additional information.
7. Click Close | OK.

Business Contact Manager is really particular about the format of the data for an import into Products and Services. Be sure to click the Help button during the Import wizard and read the section on the proper format for your import file. Also, you cannot import into the Unit cost or Taxable fields, so you will have to manually update that data once you have imported the list.

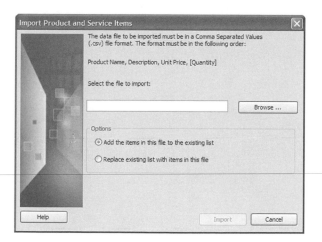

Chapter 8

Writing Letters and Campaigns

- Creating a mail merge in Microsoft Word
- Implementing marketing campaigns

Creating a mail merge in Microsoft Word

Facilitating communication with customers and prospects is an important feature of any contact management system. A mail merge allows you to send the same communication, whether it is a letter, e-mail message, or flyer, to multiple contacts, and you can personalize each communication with data from the contact's record in your database.

Task A   Creating a mail merge template

Using Microsoft Word, you can create mail merge templates. You can then select business contacts from Business Contact Manager. Using embedded field placeholders in the template, you can complete the merge to produce personalized letters for multiple contacts at once.

The Microsoft Office button is new to Office 2007 and this new button appears in the upper-left corner of many Office applications, including Outlook, Business Contact Manager, Word, and more. When you click on this button, you will see a list of commands, most of which used to be available from the File drop-down menu in older versions of Word.

To create a mail merge template:

1. Open Microsoft Word by clicking Start | All Programs | Microsoft Office | Microsoft Office Word 2007.
2. Click on the Mailings tab on the ribbon. Then in the Start Mail Merge group on the ribbon, click Start Mail Merge and select the type of document you are going to use for your mail merge. In this example we will create a Normal Word document.
3. Enter the contents of the letter, and then click on the Microsoft Office button, click Save As, and select Word Template.
4. In the File name area, put in the name for this template and click Save. For this example, we will save this template as "New Product Launch Letter."

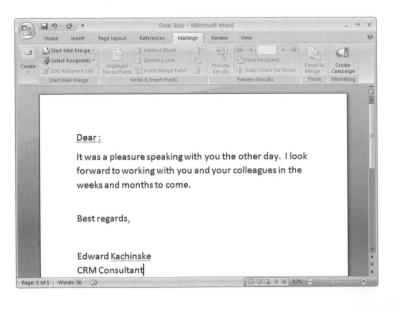

Task B Choosing contacts to include in the mail merge

Using the tight integration between Microsoft Word and Business Contact Manager, you can select business contacts from your Business Contact Manager database to include in a mail merge. All of this happens right from the Mailings tab on the ribbon in Word.

To choose contacts to include in the mail merge:

1. In Microsoft Word, open the template. See the previous task for instructions on creating a template.
2. Click on the Mailings tab at the top. In the Start Mail Merge group on the ribbon, click Select Recipients | Select from Microsoft Outlook Contacts | Business Contacts | OK. Note that you can select recipients from both your Outlook contacts and your Business Contact Manager business contacts.
3. The business contacts with a check mark in the check box column will be included in the mail merge. To deselect all business contacts, clear the check mark in the check box column header. To select all business contacts, click in the check box on the check box column.
4. Once you have selected the business contacts you want to include on the mail merge, click OK.
5. Click on the Microsoft Office button and click Save.

Have you ever received a letter addressed to "Occupant"? Chances are that letter didn't make it out of the envelope it arrived in, and it was fast-tracked to the "round file" or trash can. The key to an effective mail merge is personalization. Even simple things, like using a first name in the greeting, can increase the chance that your communication will be read. And your customers and prospects can't act on an offer or information about your products and services if they don't ever read about them.

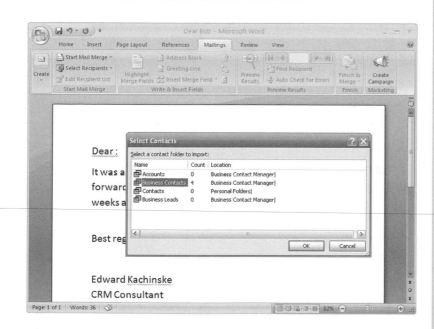

Filtering contacts to include in the mail merge

If you only have a handful of contacts, then manually selecting those contacts to whom you want to send a mail merge is easy. But if you have more than 15-20 contacts, that manual selection starts to get tricky. Also, you might want to select mail merge recipients based on some criteria of your business contacts, such as all prospects or customers in a particular state or territory. Using the filtering option when selecting business contacts to include in your mail merge makes it easy to deliver targeted communication to your customers and prospects.

To filter the contacts to include in the mail merge:

1. If you are not in Microsoft Word, click Start | All Programs | Microsoft Office | Microsoft Office Word 2007.
2. Click on the Microsoft Office button and click Open. Then select the template you saved in the last task and click Open.
3. Click on the Mailings tab at the top, and in the Start Mail Merge group on the ribbon, click Select Recipients | Select from Microsoft Outlook Contacts | Business Contacts | OK.
4. In the Refine recipient list section, click Filter.
5. In the Filter and Sort dialog box, click in the first Field drop-down, and select a field by which to filter your mail merge recipients. For this example, we will filter to find all of the business contacts that have an address. Choose the Address field.
6. In the Comparison field, change the drop-down from the default Equal to and select Is not blank, and then click OK.
7. Back in the Mail Merge Recipients dialog box, you should now be looking at a subset of your business contacts, which are all the business contacts with data in the address fields.
8. Click on the Microsoft Office button and click Save.

Once you have added the mail merge recipients for your template, the next time you open this template you will receive a warning that "Opening this document will run the following SQL command:" This is part of the new security restrictions in Office 2007. If this were a file you had gotten from someone else, you might want to click the No button in response to the "Do you want to continue?" question, but since this a template that we just created, go ahead and click the Yes button.

Task D Adding mail merge fields to the template

The power of a mail merge communication is in the ability to personalize that communication. Including field placeholders allows you to individually address and greet your customers and prospects by name, but still take advantage of the productivity and time-savings of a mass mailing. You can insert field place-holders on your Word mail merge template, and when you complete the merge, your business contact's unique information will be pulled from his record in Business Contact Manager and merged into the Word template.

To add mail merge fields to the template:

1. If you are not in Microsoft Word, click Start | All Programs | Microsoft Office | Microsoft Office Word 2007.

2. Click on the Microsoft Office button and click Open. Then select the template you saved in the last task and click Open. When you see the warning, click Yes to continue opening the document.

3. Now we can start adding mail merge fields to our template, and we will start with a date and the business contact's address block and greeting. Click on the Insert tab and in the Text group on the ribbon, click Date & Time. Choose the date format you want to use and be sure to click the Update automatically check box, then click OK.

4. Press Enter twice to insert some blank lines between the date and the address block, then click on the Mailings tab, and in the Write & Insert Fields group on the ribbon, click Address Block. Select the Address Elements, choose the business contact name format and if the Preview of the address block looks good, click OK.

5. Press Enter twice to insert some blank lines between the date and the address block and the next section of the mail merge template. In the Write & Insert Fields group on the ribbon, click Greeting Line and select the format of the greeting. Notice that if a recipient is missing a name, the mail merge template will insert a generic greeting. If the Preview of the greeting line looks good, click OK.

6. Press Enter twice to insert some blank lines between the greeting line and the body of the letter. Enter the text for the body of the letter, and then enter your signature block.

7. Click on the Microsoft Office button and click Save.

You can see what the final product will look like before actually printing or clicking the Send button. On the Mailings tab, in the Preview Results group on the ribbon, click the Preview Results button. You can then view exactly how the merged document will look with data from your business contacts, checking that the formatting is correct and that the field placeholders work properly.

If you need to create a mail merge for just a single business contact, you use the same mail merge function process described in this chapter, but when you get to the Filter recipients option, you can filter by the business contact's last name.

Task E   Completing the mail merge

To create a mail merge, you need to first create a template, then select the business contacts to which you would like to send the communication from Business Contact Manager, add the field placeholders to personalize the communication, and then finally perform the mail merge itself. The nice part is that once you have created a template, you can re-use it repeatedly.

To complete the mail merge:

1. If you are not in Microsoft Word, click Start | All Programs | Microsoft Office | Microsoft Office Word 2007.

2. Click on the Microsoft Office button and click Open. Then select the template you saved in the last task and click Open. When you see the warning, click Yes to continue opening the document.

3. Confirm that the recipients will be from Business Contact Manager and click OK.

4. The mail merge will open, previewing the results with your selected business contact recipients.

5. On the Mailings tab, in the Finish group on the ribbon, click Finish & Merge.

6. Select how you want to produce this document; for this task, we will choose Edit Individual Documents and click OK to merge all selected records.

7. You will then be in a new Word document, with the merged letter to all of your business contact recipients. You can now print and save this document as you would normally.

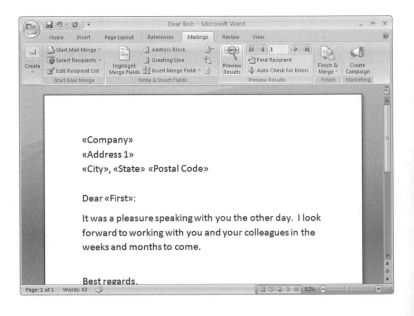

Implementing marketing campaigns

Sending marketing communication to your customers and prospects is important, but if it's a one-off mailing that you send and then forget, then it might not be the most effective method of building your business. Using Business Contact Manager's marketing campaign feature allows you to create a series of communication and track the results, including some basic ROI (return on investment) information.

Task A Creating a marketing campaign for selected accounts or business contacts

The key to an effective marketing campaign is creating a specific, targeted list of accounts or business contacts from your Business Contact Manager database for that campaign. You might want to target contacts in a specific geographic area, or contacts that you have rated "good" or "excellent" in Business Contact Manager. Thinking through the goal of the marketing campaign should help you to target the list of accounts or business contacts to include in the marketing campaign.

To create a marketing campaign for selected accounts or business contacts:

1. Open Outlook and click Business Contact Manager | Business Contacts. Filter your business contacts view to just contain the contacts that should be included in the campaign.
2. Click Edit | Select All or Ctrl + A.
3. Right-click anywhere on the list and click Create | New Marketing Campaign for Business Contact(s).
4. In the What is this Marketing Campaign for section, enter the title of the marketing campaign and a campaign code. In the Campaign type drop-down, select Direct Mail Print.
5. In the Who will see it section, the Already created radio button should be selected.
6. In the How will they get it section, you can select the delivery method. Because we selected the direct mail print as the campaign type, our selection of the delivery method is limited to either a Word or Publisher mail merge. For this exercise, we'll select the Word mail merge.
7. In the What will they get section, click the Browse button, and select a document or template and click Open.
8. In the Are you ready to launch the Marketing Campaign section, click Launch.

In this example, we are targeting our prospects. You can easily indicate and find contacts that are prospects by using the categorization function of Business Contact Manager. Assigning categories to your business contacts is very powerful. We covered categorization in detail in Chapter 4.

9. On the Mailings tab, in the Finish group on the ribbon, click Finish & Merge.

10. Select how you want to produce this document. For this example, we'll choose Edit Individual Documents and click OK to merge all selected records.

11. You will then be in a new Word document, with the merged letter to all of your business contact recipients. You can now print and save this document as you would normally.

Task B   Creating a marketing campaign using search folders

Search folders are an excellent tool that can be used to hold different types of contacts in a list. When you customize a particular view in Business Contact Manager by applying filters, you are generating a targeted list that you can use in a marketing campaign. The only downside is that those views are not always sticky, meaning that when you next view your list of business contacts in Business Contact Manager, the filters will be gone, and you will be viewing your entire business contact list. You can save those customized views that filter a subset of your business contacts by using search folders.

To create a marketing campaign using search folders:

1. Filter your business contacts list to show just the contacts that should be included in this campaign. Highlight all of the contacts.
2. Right-click anywhere on the list and click Create | New Marketing Campaign for Business Contact(s).
3. In the What is this Marketing Campaign for section, enter the title of the marketing campaign and a campaign code. These two fields are required when creating a new marketing campaign. You can also choose the campaign type, start and end dates, budgeted cost, and comments. For this task we will choose Direct Mail Print as the Campaign type.
4. In the Who will see it section, the Already created radio button should be selected.
5. In the How will they get it section, you can select the delivery method.
6. In the What will they get section, click the Browse button and select a document or template and click Open.
7. In the Are you ready to launch the Marketing Campaign section, click Launch.
8. On the Mailings tab, in the Finish group on the ribbon, click Finish & Merge.
9. Select how you want to produce this document. For this example, we will choose Edit Individual Documents and click OK to merge all selected records.
10. You will then be in a new Word document, with the merged letter to all of your business contact recipients. You can now print and save this document as you would normally.

Search folders are very flexible and powerful ways of quickly grouping business contacts. You can create multiple search folders and use them to view a selected portion of your business contacts. When you add a new contact to your Business Contact Manager database, if any of the fields in that new business contact record match the filter options for one of your search folders, that contact will be added automatically to that search folder.

Task C   Creating a marketing campaign from a report

Running and viewing reports is a good way to analyze the business contacts in your Business Contact Manager database. Often the output of a report might be the perfect launching point for a new marketing campaign. You can actually create a new marketing campaign right from the preview of a Business Contact Manager report.

Reports are an important function of any contact management system. They let you view and analyze the data in your database so that you can make more effective decisions and choices about your marketing, sales, products, and services. We cover reports in detail in Chapter 11.

To create a marketing campaign from a report:

1. Click Business Contact Manager | Report | Business Contacts | Business Contact by State/Province (or choose a different report).
2. Click Actions | Filter Report.
3. To filter the report to show only contacts in a particular state or states, click Advanced Filter and in the field name drop-down, select Business State/Province.
4. Click Actions | Launch Marketing Campaign and click Selected Items. This creates a new marketing campaign only for the business contacts that you selected via the filter. If you select All Items, Business Contact Manager will launch the marketing campaign for all the business contacts on the report.
5. Enter the title of the marketing campaign and a campaign code.
6. In the How will they get it section, you can select the delivery method.
7. In the What will they get section, click the Browse button and select a document or template and click Open.
8. Repeat steps 7-10 in Task B above.

Task D   Creating a marketing campaign in Word

One of the nice things about Business Contact Manager is the tight relationship between Business Contact Manager and the other Microsoft Office products, like Word.

Earlier in the chapter, we reviewed how from within Microsoft Word you could create mail merge templates, then select business contacts from Business Contact Manager, embed field placeholders from Business Contact Manager into the mail merge template, and complete the mail merge. You can also create a new marketing campaign at the same time.

To create a marketing campaign in Word:

1. Open Microsoft Word by clicking Start | All Programs | Microsoft Office | Microsoft Office Word 2007.

2. Create and save your campaign document. For this example, we'll create a mail merge template for an e-mail message. See the task earlier in this chapter for the steps to create a mail merge template.

3. Click on the Mailings tab, then in the Marketing group on the ribbon, click Create Campaign. Because you created the campaign in Word, some of the campaign information has already been filled in, but you can edit and add to the campaign.

4. In the Who will see it section, the Select from these options radio button will be selected and Custom List will be in the drop-down. You can click on that drop-down and select another list, including business contacts in a search folder.

5. In the How will they get it section, you can select the delivery method.

6. In the What will they get section, the Use existing file field should be populated with the e-mail mail merge template you created.

7. In the Are you ready to launch the Marketing Campaign section, click Launch.

8. On the Mailings tab, in the Finish group on the ribbon, click Finish & Merge and select Send E-mail Messages.

9. In the Merge to E-mail dialog box, enter the Subject line for each e-mail, and choose the Mail format. For an e-mail, you will likely select HTML. Click OK to merge all selected records.

10. Your e-mail mail merge is sent to the Outlook Outbox, and will eventually appear in your Sent Items folder.

When you are in Microsoft Word, you can create a marketing campaign and select business contacts from Business Contact Manager to include in that campaign. Because you created the campaign from Word, much of the campaign details will be filled out, like the title of the campaign, the type (Direct Mail Print), and the delivery method (Word Mail Merge).

Creating a marketing campaign in Publisher

Once again we see the benefits of the close integration between Business Contact Manager and the rest of the Microsoft Office family of products. You can create a publication using Microsoft Publisher, and then right in Publisher, you can create a new marketing campaign so that you can track the results of your marketing efforts.

To create a marketing campaign in Publisher:

1. Open Publisher by clicking Start | All Programs | Microsoft Office | Microsoft Office Publisher 2007.

2. Create and save a publication, such as a flyer.

3. You need to make sure you can see the Business Contact Manager toolbar in Publisher. Click View | Toolbars | Business Contact Manager. Then on the Business Contact Manager toolbar, click Create New Marketing Campaign. Because you created the campaign in Publisher, some of the campaign information has already been filled in, but you can edit and add to the campaign.

4. In the Who will see it section, you can select which contacts will be included in the campaign.

5. In the How will they get it section, you can select the delivery method. Because we created the campaign from a flyer in Publisher, the delivery method of Publisher Mail Merge is already selected for you.

6. In the What will they get section, the Use existing file field should be populated with the publication you created.

7. In the Are you ready to launch the Marketing Campaign section, click Launch.

8. On the Mail Merge Navigation Pane on the left-hand side of the screen, you can add Business Contact Manager fields to the publication, as well as find and edit recipients. Click Next | Create merged publication.

9. In the Create merged publication section, you can click Merge to a new publication. You can then print and save this publication as you would normally.

10. Your e-mail mail merge is sent to the Outlook Outbox, and it will eventually appear in your Sent Items folder.

Although Microsoft touts the "seamless" integration among the Microsoft suite of Office products, we didn't really get the seamless part in working with Publisher. For one, Publisher 2007 retains much of the older look and feel of Office programs, lacking the ribbon and Microsoft button functionality. Creating and performing an e-mail mail merge from Publisher was also less than intuitive, and we found working with Microsoft Word to be much easier. So unless you are already a Publisher pro, or you need advanced design for your marketing pieces, we recommend sticking to Microsoft Word.

Task F Using the Outlook e-mail marketing service

E-mail marketing is here to stay, and if you plan to do any marketing through this communication channel, it's worth looking at the Outlook e-mail marketing service. The service provides some extremely useful tools for tracking things like the number of bounced e-mail messages, the number of contacts that unsubscribed, the number of business contacts that clicked on any links in your e-mail, and the number of replies. This kind of feedback is crucial to creating truly valuable and effective e-mail marketing communications.

To use the Outlook e-mail marketing service:

1. Open Microsoft Word by clicking Start | All Programs | Microsoft Office | Microsoft Office Word 2007.
2. Create and save your campaign document. For this example, we'll create a mail merge template for an e-mail message. See the task earlier in this chapter for the steps to create a mail merge template.
3. In the Marketing group on the ribbon, click Create Campaign. Because you created the campaign in Word, some of the campaign information has already been filled in, but you can edit it and add to the campaign.
4. In the Who will see it section, the Select from these options radio button will be selected and Custom List will be in the drop-down. You can click on that drop-down and select another list, including business contacts in a search folder.
5. In the How will they get it section, you can select the delivery method. Select the E-mail Marketing Service.
6. In the What will they get section, the Use existing file field should be populated with the e-mail mail merge template you created.
7. In the Are you ready to launch the Marketing Campaign section, click Launch.
8. When the E-mail Marketing Service wizard opens, complete the steps in the wizard to send your e-mail via the service.

The Outlook e-mail marketing service also performs another valuable function by sending all of the e-mail messages in a marketing campaign or e-mail mail merge through the Microsoft servers. Many ISPs (Internet Service Providers) limit the amount of bulk mail that can be sent through their mail servers. Because the e-mail messages sent through the Outlook e-mail marketing service don't ever hit your ISP's servers, you can avoid this limitation. And as a Business Contact Manager user, you can send 50 messages per month, free. You can increase that amount by subscribing to a plan allowing 1,000 or 10,000 e-mail messages per month.

Task G Tracking the results of a marketing campaign

Marketing campaigns are an effective tool for creating, sending, and tracking marketing communication to your business contacts. When it comes to marketing campaigns, tracking is where the rubber meets the road.

You can track the marketing campaign results for the following:
- Leads
- Opportunities
- Accounts
- Business Contacts

To track the results of a marketing campaign:

1. Click Business Contact Manager | Marketing Campaigns and double-click a campaign that has been executed to view the tracking options.

2. In the Show group on the ribbon, click Track.

3. This will show you the campaign results, including total leads, opportunities, accounts, and contacts, as well as the list of recipients.

4. You can enter the actual cost of the campaign.

5. To populate the campaign results, you will need to enter the campaign code on the Business Contact Manager record.

6. Click Business Contact Manager | Business Contacts and double-click a business contact to update the campaign information.

7. In the Source information area, click the Initiated By button. In the Folder drop-down, select Marketing Campaigns and then select the marketing campaign and click Link To or double-click the campaign, then click OK. Now when you return to the marketing campaign record, you can see the results. To see more detail on the specific results for leads, opportunities, accounts, or contacts, click the Show Report button.

8. Click Save & Close.

Chapter 9

E-mail

- Sending e-mails to a business contact
- Auto-linking

Sending e-mails to a business contact

How many e-mail messages do you send in a typical day? How many appear in your Inbox? Chances are much of the communication you have with customers, prospects, vendors, suppliers, and other business contacts in your Business Contact Manager database is via e-mail. Using Business Contact Manager to track that communication is critical to effectively managing the relationships with your business contacts.

Task A   Sending an e-mail to a business contact

You can send an e-mail message to a business contact, and if you initiate that e-mail message from the business contact record in Business Contact Manager, that message will be linked to the business contact record so that you can refer back to it from the business contact record. The messages you send from a business contact are stored in the History view on a business contact.

To send an e-mail to a business contact:

1. Go to your list of business contacts. You can get there by clicking Business Contact Manager | Business Contacts.
2. Select the business contact by clicking once on the contact.
3. Click Actions | Create | New Message to Business Contact.
4. Enter the subject and the body of the e-mail message and click Send.
5. The e-mail will now appear on the History view for that business contact.

If you initiate sending an e-mail message from a business contact record, Business Contact Manager will automatically link that e-mail message to that business contact so that you can view that e-mail message from that business contact's record in the History view.

Linking a previously sent e-mail message to a Business Contact Manager record

If you didn't initiate an e-mail message from the business contact record, you can still go back to your Sent Items folder in Outlook and link that e-mail message to the business contact record. Then you can view that e-mail message from that business contact's record in the History view.

To link a previously sent e-mail message to a Business Contact Manager record:

1. In the Outlook Navigation Pane, click Mail, and then click on the Sent Items folder. For this example, we will link a previously sent e-mail message with a business contact, but these steps apply to any record type in Business Contact Manager.

2. Right-click the message you would like to link with a business contact and click Link to Record.

3. This will open the Link to Business Contact Manager record dialog box. In the Folder drop-down, select Business Contacts. A list of your business contacts appears. You can either search for a name in the Search box by typing the first or last name of the business contact or click on a name in the list.

4. Click Link To to add that business contact to the Linked Records box and click OK. Or, you can double-click the business contact name, which will populate the Link To box, then click OK.

You can link e-mail messages to the following record types in Business Contact Manager:

- Accounts
- Business Contacts
- Opportunities
- Business Projects

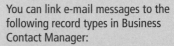

Link to Business Contact Manager record

| Search: | | Folder: |
| | | Business Contacts |

Full Name	File As	Company
Betty Bing	Bing, Betty	Bing's Bling
Carol Gilliland	Gilliland, Carol	Power of 3 Consulting
Edward Kachinske	Kachinske, Edward	Innovative Solutions CRM
Stacy Roach	Roach, Stacy	Power of 3 Consulting
Steve Stroz	Stroz, Steve	Gold Coast Advisors
Timothy Kachinske	Kachinske, Timothy	Innovative Solutions

Linked Records

Link To -> Carol Gilliland;

New... Open...

OK Cancel

The manual linking of e-mail messages, either from your Inbox or Sent Items folders, can only be done one e-mail message at a time. If you want to link all the e-mail messages in your Inbox folder to a particular business contact, then you should use the e-mail auto-link function, which is discussed later in this chapter.

Task C   Linking items in your Inbox to a business contact

Given that e-mail communication is a two-way street, you want to be sure to link any incoming e-mail messages to a Business Contact Manager record, as well as linking outgoing and/or previously sent e-mail messages.

To link items in your Inbox to a business contact:

1. In the Outlook Navigation Pane, click Mail and then click on the Inbox folder. For this example, we will link an e-mail message in our Inbox to an opportunity, but these steps apply to any record type in Business Contact Manager.

2. Right-click the message you would like to link with an opportunity and click Link to Record.

3. This will open the Link to Business Contact Manager record dialog box. In the Folder drop-down, select Opportunities. A list of your opportunities will display. You can either search for an opportunity title or Associated Account or business contact in the Search box by typing part of the business project name or clicking on an opportunity in the list.

4. Click Link To to add that opportunity to the Linked Records box and click OK. Or you can double-click the business contact name, which will populate the Link to box, then click OK.

Task D Linking an e-mail message to a business project

Linking e-mail messages to business contacts is important, but you may also want to link an e-mail message to a business project so that you can view all the history of e-mail communication associated with a given business project.

To link an e-mail message to a business project:

1. In the Outlook Navigation Pane, click Mail and then click on the Inbox folder.
2. Right-click the message you would like to link with a business project and click Link to Record.
3. This will open the Link to Business Contact Manager record dialog box. In the Folder drop-down, select Business Projects. A list of your business projects will display. You can either search for a Project Name or Associated Account or Business Contact in the Search box by typing part of the business project name or clicking on an opportunity in the list.
4. Click Link To to add that opportunity to the Linked Records box and click OK. Or you can double-click the business contact name, which will populate the Link to box, then click OK.

Auto-linking

The e-mail auto-linking feature of Business Contact Manager is an important, powerful, and time-saving feature. When you initiate auto-linking, all of the e-mail messages, including meeting requests and assigned tasks, will be automatically linked to that business contact. This ensures that all of the e-mail communication, both incoming and outgoing, with your business contacts will be saved to the History view, providing you with a complete overview of the interaction with your business contacts. Auto-linking also provides a mechanism for quickly adding new business contacts to your Business Contact Manager database.

The e-mail auto-link feature is both a powerful feature of Business Contact Manager and a big timesaver, but there are two areas of caution to note:

First, given that you can only manually link one e-mail message at a time, the auto-link will save you that tedious task. The only downside is that every incoming and outgoing e-mail message will now be linked to an existing Business Contact Manager business contact or business project. This means that even non-substantive e-mail exchanges will all be in the History view of a business contact or business project. This can make it difficult to weed through a large volume of e-mail messages to find relevant information.

Second, sharing is nice, but you should be aware that when you initiate the e-mail auto-link feature in a shared database, all of the users of that database would be able to view any of the e-mail messages that are automatically linked to an account, business contact, or business project.

Task A   Auto-linking e-mail messages from a business contact record

The e-mail auto-link feature can be initiated from a business contact or from an incoming or sent e-mail message. In this task we will set up an e-mail auto-link from a business contact record.

To auto-link e-mail messages from a business contact record:

1. Go to your list of business contacts. You can get there by clicking Business Contact Manager | Business Contacts.
2. Double-click the business contact to open that record.
3. In the Options group on the ribbon, click E-mail Auto-link.
4. Make sure that the Link box is checked for the business contact and click OK.
5. Now all of your future incoming and outgoing e-mail messages will be auto-linked with that business contact.

Task B   Auto-linking e-mail messages from an account record

The e-mail auto-link feature can be initiated from a business contact or from an incoming or sent e-mail message. In this task, we will set up the e-mail auto-link from a business contact record.

To auto-link e-mail messages from an account record:

1. Go to your list of accounts by clicking Business Contact Manager | Accounts.
2. Double-click an account to open that record.
3. In the Options group on the ribbon, click E-mail Auto-link.
4. Make sure that the Link box is checked for the account and click OK.
5. Now all of your future incoming and outgoing e-mail messages will be auto-linked with that account.

When you initiate e-mail auto-linking for an account, Business Contact Manager includes all of the business contacts that are listed with that account, provided that all the business contacts have an e-mail address in their record.

When you initiate the e-mail auto-link feature, only messages sent and received from that point forward will be auto-linked to the account, business contact, or business project. There is a Search and Link function of Business Contact Manager that will search your e-mail message folders and link all the incoming and sent e-mail messages to the business contact or business project. That function is discussed later in this chapter.

Task C   Auto-linking e-mail messages from an incoming e-mail message

If you are like most people, when you open Outlook, you probably read through your new e-mail messages in your Inbox, rather than going to your business contact or account list in Business Contact Manager. If you see an e-mail message and you would like to use that incoming message to set up the e-mail auto-link feature, you can quickly and easily do that, right from the comfort of your Inbox.

To auto-link e-mail messages to a business contact from an incoming e-mail message:

1. In the Outlook Navigation Pane, click Mail and then click on the Inbox folder. For this example, we will create an e-mail auto-link from an e-mail message in your Inbox with a business contact, but these steps also apply to setting up the auto-link function for an account or business project as well.

2. Right-click the message from the contact with whom you would like to set up the e-mail auto-link function and click E-mail Auto-link.

3. This will open the E-mail Auto-link to Business Contact Manager record dialog box. On the E-mail Address tab, make sure that the Link check box is checked for the business contact for which you would like to set up the e-mail auto-link function and click OK.

Task D   Auto-linking e-mail messages with a business project

You can set up the e-mail auto-link feature for a business project in addition to setting up that function for business contacts. Business Contact Manager uses the subject line entry of your e-mail when auto-linking e-mail messages to business projects. E-mail auto-linking to an opportunity is not supported in Business Contact Manager.

To auto-link e-mail messages with a business project:

1. In the Outlook Navigation Pane, click Mail, and then click on the Inbox folder.
2. Right-click the message and click E-mail Auto-link
3. Click on the Business Contact Manager Projects tab and click the check box for the business project for which you want to set up the auto-link function.
4. Click OK.

When you apply the e-mail auto-link feature to a business project, the auto-linking is managed only by the e-mail's subject. Let's say you set up a business project to manage your company's website redesign and you want to auto-link any e-mails that pertain to that project. If you set up the auto-link feature on an e-mail with the subject "Website Redesign," then the only incoming or sent e-mail messages that will be auto-linked to the business project will be those with the subject "Website Redesign." An e-mail message from your web designer with the subject "Website Design Review," for example, would not be auto-linked, unless you also set up an e-mail auto-link for that incoming e-mail message, which would add that e-mail subject to the auto-link function for that business project.

Task E   Managing e-mail auto-link options

You can manage the e-mail auto-linking function to control the e-mail addresses you have auto-linked as well as the Outlook folders you would like to scan for auto-linking. In addition, from the Manage E-mail Auto-linking dialog box, you can have Business Contact Manager search messages in your Outlook folders and link them to the relevant business contacts and/or business projects.

To manage e-mail auto-link options:

1. Click Business Contact Manager | Manage E-mail Auto-linking.
2. This will bring up the Manage E-mail Auto-linking dialog box.
3. On the E-mail tab, you can manage all of the contacts for which you are currently auto-linking e-mail messages. To turn off auto-link for a business contact, just uncheck the box under the Link column. You can also Clear All to turn off the auto-link feature for all business contacts.
4. On the Folders tab, you can select which folders in Outlook you want to have Business Contact Manager monitor for auto-linking. If you have created folders in Outlook, you need make sure the e-mail messages in those folders are also included in the auto-link function. Business Contact Manager will not automatically select those subfolders—this prevents folders you did not intend to include in the auto-link function from being scanned for e-mail messages.
5. At the bottom of the dialog box, click the Search and Link button to have Business Contact Manager scan the folders you selected and auto-link any e-mail messages to your business contacts. You can set the Search function to ignore older messages by checking the Ignore e-mail older than check box and entering a date. Then click Start. Depending on how far back you are searching and linking, this process could take a while.
6. Click OK.

There is a preference setting in Outlook that needs to be set in order for the e-mail auto-link feature in Business Contact Manager to be able to scan your sent items and auto-link e-mail messages in that folder. In Outlook, click Tools | Options | Preferences | E-mail Options. Make sure that the Save messages in Sent Items folder check box is checked. It is checked by default, but Business Contact Manager does not scan your Outbox to auto-link e-mail messages, just your sent items.

Task F Unlinking an e-mail message from a record

When you set up the e-mail auto-link feature, Business Contact Manager will link every e-mail message, including meeting requests and assigned tasks, to the account, business contact, or business project. You may find an e-mail message or two that don't need to be linked to the Business Contact Manager record, and in that case, you can easily unlink that message from the account, business contact, or business project that it was automatically linked to originally.

To unlink an e-mail message from a record:

1. In this example, we will unlink an e-mail message from a business contact, but the same steps apply to accounts and business projects. Go to your list of business contacts. You can get there by clicking Business Contact Manager | Business Contacts.
2. Open the business contact by double-clicking on the contact.
3. In the Show group of the ribbon, click History.
4. Right-click the e-mail message to unlink from this business contact and select Delete.

When you are unlinking an e-mail message from an account, a business contact, or a business project, you use the Delete command. This can be a little scary and you might be wondering if it will delete the actual e-mail message itself from the folder in Outlook. Rest assured, the e-mail message will be in Outlook until you delete it from there.

Creating a new business contact from an incoming e-mail message using the e-mail auto-link feature involves a couple of steps, but this method allows you to quickly create a new business contact from an incoming e-mail message and initiate the e-mail auto-link feature for that business contact's e-mail address. Because the e-mail message header typically holds very little contact information, like company, phone, address, etc., you will need to take the extra step of opening and editing the business contacts created via this method and updating their business contact record more fully.

Task G   Using the e-mail auto-link feature to create new business contacts

When you are in your Outlook Inbox reading your incoming e-mail messages, you will likely find an e-mail message from someone who is not a business contact in your Business Contact Manager database. You can quickly create a new business contact from that incoming e-mail message and set up the e-mail auto-link feature at the same time. The information on the business contact record will be sparse when you use this method, so it will require you, at some point, to open the business contact record and fill in any missing information, like company name, phone, address, etc.

To use the e-mail auto-link feature to create a new business contact:

1. In the Outlook Navigation Pane, click Mail and then click on the Inbox folder.
2. Right-click the message and click E-mail Auto-link.
3. On the E-mail Address tab, you will see a list of all of the e-mail addresses in that message, including any e-mail addresses in the Cc line of the message.
4. Click in the Link check box to select the e-mail addresses for which you want to create new business contacts and click OK. This will create a business contact record in Business Contact Manager.
5. Now go to your business contacts by clicking Business Contact Manager | Business Contacts. Open the record for the business contact you just created. The information in the new business contact record is taken from that business contact's e-mail, and it will probably be lacking quite a bit of information. You can fill out the rest of the information for this business contact then click Save.
6. Auto-linking will be set up for this new business contact. In the Options group on the ribbon, click E-mail Auto-link, the Link check box will be selected, and in the Type column, which previously showed as unknown, it will now indicate that this is a business contact.

Chapter 10

Managing Projects

- Creating a project
- Working with project tasks
- Tracking business projects

Creating a project

Task A Adding a new project

Most businesses and organizations need to manage projects. Whether the project is an event you need to plan, a client project, or an internal project for your business, Business Contact Manager has a tool to help you more effectively manage those projects. When you create business projects, you can enter and track project tasks and link projects to accounts and/or business contacts. The business project function of Business Contact Manager helps you manage the progress and status of the overall project, as well as the individual project tasks.

To add a new project:

1. Click Business Contact Manager | Business Projects.
2. Click Actions | New Business Project or right-click on the list of business projects and click New Business Project.
3. In the Project information section, assign a project name.
4. You can share your Business Contact Manager database with other folks in your company or organization. We cover how to share a Business Contact Manager database in Chapter 1. If you have shared your Business Contact Manager database, you can assign the project to a different Business Contact Manager user by clicking the Assigned to drop-down.
5. In the Project type drop-down, select the project type, or click the Edit this list option at the bottom of the drop-down to add a new project type.
6. In the Linked account or business contact section, you must link a business project to either an account or business contact.
7. Click the Link To button. This will open the Link to an Account or Business Contact dialog box. For this example, we will use a business contact. In the Folder drop-down, select Business Contacts. A list of your business contacts appears. You can either search for a name in the Search box by typing the first and last name of the business contact or click on a name in the list.
8. Click Link To to add that business contact to the Linked Records box and click OK. Or you can double-click the business contact name, which will populate the Link To box, then click OK.
9. Click Save & Close.

Starting a new project only requires two pieces of information: you must enter a project name and link the project to an account or business contact. There is a lot of other information you can track, but getting started with business projects is quick and easy.

You can only link a project to one type of Business Contact Manager record. So if you link a project to an account, you can't also link that project to a specific business contact. You can specify related accounts and business contacts in the project form, though, and we show you that in the next task.

Task B Entering information about a project

Beyond a project name and which account or business contact that project is linked to, you can track a whole slew of information about a project. This includes detailed information about the start and due dates, the project status, the priority of the project, and the overall percentage complete. In addition, using the Details view of the business project, you can add general comments about the project.

To enter information about a project:

1. Click Business Contact Manager | Business Projects and double-click the project you want to open.
2. In the Status information area, you can set a start and due date for the project, indicate the project status, priority, and percentage complete.
3. In the Related accounts and business contacts area, you can link multiple business contacts or accounts. To remove an account or business contact from the related accounts and business contacts area, click on the Name and then click the Remove button.
4. In the Show group on the ribbon, click Details. You can enter comments about the business project here. If you click the Add Time Stamp button before entering a comment, Business Contact Manager will insert a date and time stamp so that you can track when each comment was added.
5. When you are finished entering information about the business project, click Save & Close.

The first several lines of comments on the Details view of the business project can be displayed in the Business Projects list view when you enable the AutoPreview function. To do that, right-click anywhere in the white space on the business project list and choose AutoPreview.

You can use these comments in the Detail view of the business project to enter noteworthy information about the project, which can then be viewed in the business project list with the AutoPreview function enabled.

Task C Editing an existing project

Creating a project is quick and easy, and so is editing an existing project. Projects tend to change over the life of the project, so editing the business project record is vital to your project management efforts.

To edit an existing project:

1. Click Business Contact Manager | Business Projects and double-click the project to open it.
2. You can now add or edit any information on the General view of the business project, or click on the Details icon in the Show group on the ribbon to add and/or edit comments about the business project.
3. You can also add or remove related account and business contacts from the project.
4. When you are finished editing the business project, click Save & Close.

Task D Deleting a project

Deleting a project is as simple as adding a new business project. If you have a shared Business Contact Manager database, keep in mind that any user can delete a business project. This is one reason that regularly backing up your Business Contact Manager is so critical. We cover database backup in Chapter 15.

To delete a project:

1. Click Business Contact Manager | Business Projects to display the list of business projects.
2. Right-click on the project you want to delete and select Delete.
3. The project is removed from the business project list and automatically moved to the Deleted Items folder under the Business Contact Manager folder in Outlook.

When you delete a record in Business Contact Manager, that record is not actually deleted, but it is moved to the Deleted Items folder under the Business Contact Manager folder. Deleted business contacts, accounts, opportunities, and business projects can be easily restored from that Deleted Items folder.

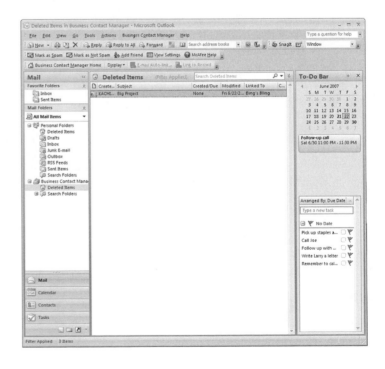

Task E Restoring a deleted project

If you accidentally delete a business project, you can restore the deleted project right from the Deleted Items folder. Deleted business projects behave the same way deleted e-mails behave in Outlook. They aren't actually deleted but are just sent to a folder pending final deletion.

To permanently delete a business project from Business Contact Manager, just delete it from the Deleted Items folder. Once an item has been deleted from the Deleted Items folder, you will not be able to recover it.

To restore a deleted project:

1. Click the Business Contact Manager Home button on the toolbar.
2. In the Navigation Pane, click the Business Contact Manager Deleted Items folder. It's probably at the bottom of your list of mail folders.
3. Click the business project you'd like to restore.
4. Right-click on the business project, select Move to Folder, select Business Projects, and click OK.
5. Click Business Contact Manager | Business Projects to display the list of business projects and your deleted project will be back in the list of business projects.

Working with project tasks

Tasks are the meat of the matter when it comes to managing projects. Projects are generally comprised of a list of tasks that need to get accomplished for the project to be successful. When you create a business project in Business Contact Manager, you can create a list of the tasks associated with that business project and assign those tasks to any authorized user. Business Contact Manager treats tasks associated with a business project differently from other tasks in Outlook or Business Contact Manager, and you can view all of your project tasks in a separate Business Contact Manager view.

Task A   Adding project tasks

Adding new tasks to a business project is quick and easy, and you can track a number of valuable details about a specific project task, such as start and due dates, the status of the task, the percentage complete, and the priority of the task. You can even mark a task as needing attention for the project manager.

To add a project task:

1. Click Business Contact Manager | Business Projects and double-click the project to open it.
2. In the Project tasks area, click the New button to add business project tasks. We cover tasks in detail in Chapter 6. You can set the subject of the task, and if you are in a shared Business Contact Manager database, you can assign the task to any of the users of that shared Business Contact Manager database.
3. In the Linked project section, note that Business Contact Manager already linked the task to your business project because we created the task from the business project record.
4. In the Project task settings section, you can enter the start and due dates of the task, the status, percentage complete, and the priority of the project task.
5. You can set a reminder for the task by clicking the Reminder check box, which will engage the reminder date and time drop-down menus.
6. You can add comments to the project task in the comments section. If you plan to add multiple comments, you might want to first click the Add Time Stamp button and Business Contact Manager will insert a date and time stamp so that you can track when comments were added to the task.
7. When you are finished adding information to the project task, click Save & Close. The task you added will appear in the list of project tasks in the business project record. Click Save & Close to exit the business project record.

Project tasks can be viewed in a few different areas of Outlook and Business Contact Manager. Because some views include all tasks from Outlook, Business Contact Manager, and business projects, we recommend categorizing your project tasks so that you can easily filter other task views to clearly show the project-related tasks. We cover categorization in Chapter 4.

In other areas of Business Contact Manager, tasks associated with a business contact or opportunity appear as communication history items. This is not the case with business projects and project tasks. Project tasks appear on the business project in the list of project tasks and in the Project Tasks view in Business Contact Manager. Project tasks do appear on the History view of all of the accounts and/or business contacts linked to that project.

Task B   Completing project tasks

You can open and edit a project task to show progress on that task. You can update information like the percentage completion for a project task, if the task requires the attention of the project manager, and any relevant comments about the task. When the task is complete, you will want to open the task and update the status to reflect that it is completed.

To complete a project task:

1. Click Business Contact Manager | Business Projects and double-click the project to open it.
2. In the Project tasks area, double-click the project task you have completed to open that task.
3. In the Project task settings area, click in the Status drop-down and select Completed.
4. Click Save & Close. The project task will appear in the list of project tasks with a line through it, indicating it is a completed task and the percentage complete will be updated to show 100%.

Task C Adding communication history items for a project

Communication history items for business projects in Business Contact Manager include things like a business note, an e-mail message, or a file. By linking communication history items with a business project, you can track all of the interaction and communication that are related to that project. When you link a business project to a business contact, that business project will also appear as a communication history item on the business contact's record.

To add a communication history item for a project:

1. Click Business Contact Manager | Business Projects. This takes you to the list view of all of your business projects.

2. Double-click the business project to open the business project record. For this example, we will send an e-mail message to a business contact about the project status, but the process is basically the same for adding any new history item.

3. In the Communicate group on the ribbon, click New History Item | Mail Message.

4. Click the To button to address the e-mail message, and in Select Names, change the address book from Contacts to Business Contacts. A list of your business contacts appears. You can either search for a name in the Search box by typing the first and last name of the business contact or click on a name in the list.

5. You can also include other business contacts in this e-mail message by adding them to the To, Cc, or Bcc lines, then click OK.

6. Enter a subject, such as "Project Status" and then enter the body of the e-mail message. When you are done with the message, click Send.

You can create and link the following history items with a business project:

- Business Note
- Phone Log
- Mail Message
- Appointment
- File

Task D Viewing communication history items for a project

Communication history items for business projects in Business Contact Manager include things like a business note, an e-mail message, or a file. By linking communication history items with a business project, you can track all of the interaction and communication that is related to that business project. Viewing the communication history items for a business project provides an overview of all of the interaction related to that project.

To view communication history items for a project:

1. Click Business Contact Manager | Business Projects. This takes you to the list view of all of your business projects.

2. Double-click the business project to open the business project record, and in the Show group on the ribbon, click History.

3. You will then be viewing all of the communication history items for this project.

4. Click Save & Close.

The other place you can view the communication history item is on the linked account or business contact for that business project. Open the account or business contact record, and in the Show group on the ribbon, click History. You will be viewing all of the communication history items for that record, including those that are linked to a business project. If you select the By Linked To in the view drop-down, you will be able to see all of the communication history items for the business project, including the project tasks.

Tracking business projects

The business project record in Business Contact Manager provides an overview of all of the relevant information needed to effectively manage a project. There is a project overview that shows the number of completed, overdue, incomplete, and important tasks, as well as days left to the due date of the project. You can also view the overall project status details, and the status of individual project tasks.

Task A   Viewing and filtering projects

You can view a single business project or a list of your business projects. The standard business project views are a good start on different ways to track and analyze your projects, but by using the filtering options in the project list view, you can drill down and view, for example, specific types of projects, projects by status, or projects due within the next week.

To view and filter projects:

1. To view a specific business project, click Business Contact Manager | Business Projects. This will display a list view of all of your business projects. Double-click a business project to open that project and view the project overview, status, and project tasks.

2. To view all of your business projects, click Business Contact Manager | Business Projects. This will display a list view of all of your business projects. You can change the view in the current view section of the Outlook Navigation Pane. You can also customize the current view.

3. If you want to view only the current or in progress projects, right-click on the list view and select Customize Current View. Click Filter | Advanced | Field | User-defined fields in folder | Project Status. In the Condition drop-down, select is (exactly) and in the Value field type In Progress. Click Add to list and OK twice.

4. The filter on the business project list view is not always sticky, however, so if you switch to any other view in Outlook or Business Contact Manager, when you return to the list view of your business projects, the filter may no longer be active on that view.

In Business Contact Manager, business projects are treated like a kind of task. This makes performing some functions, like filtering the business project list view, a bit cumbersome, because the default filtering options are task-based. You just need to dig a bit deeper in the filter to find the project-related fields that you can use to filter your list of business projects.

The filtering options in many of the views in Business Contact Manager are not always sticky, which is to say that once you set the filter, when you either switch to a new view or close and re-open Business Contact Manager, the filters you set may be cleared, restoring the default view. This can be annoying, but just remember that you can create a search folder, which effectively saves your filters.

Task B   Viewing and filtering project tasks

Business Contact Manager recognizes the importance of project tasks, and it provides a specific view of project tasks. This view lets you easily track and analyze the tasks related to a project. The standard project task views include: by the user the task is assigned to, the project, by the due date of the task, or just a simple project task list. You can also customize any of the views to further drill down and filter your project task list.

To view and filter project tasks:

1. To view your business projects, click Business Contact Manager | Project Tasks. This will display a list view of all of your project tasks. You can change the view in the current view section of the Outlook navigation pane on the left. You can also customize the current view.

2. If you want to view all the project tasks that are flagged as attention required, right-click on the list view and select Customize Current View. Click Filter | Advanced | Field | User-defined fields in folder | Attention Required. In the Condition drop-down, select equals and in the Value drop-down, select Yes. Click Add to list and OK twice.

3. The filter on the project task list view is not always sticky, however, so if you switch to any other view in Outlook or Business Contact Manager, when you return to the list view of your project tasks, the filter may no longer be active on that view.

Task C Viewing the task timeline

Outlook provides a unique view of all of the To-Do's, called a Task Timeline. This view shows all of the tasks, including Outlook, Business Contact Manager, and business project tasks. The format of the view is similar to a Gantt chart, which is a very typical type of project management chart showing tasks over time. If a task is going to take a week, then that task shows as a bar crossing seven days in the task timeline view.

To view the task timeline:

1. In the Outlook Navigation Pane, click Tasks. In the My Tasks section, select To-Do List.
2. In the current view, select the Task Timeline radio button.
3. You will now be viewing a timeline of all of your tasks. This view will show you both Outlook tasks as well as Business Contact Manager and project tasks.
4. The view is similar to a Gantt chart, which is typically a bar chart showing activities over blocks of time. Gantt charts are often used in managing projects to show the project tasks over time.

The Task Timeline view displays Outlook tasks, Business Contact Manager tasks, and business project tasks. Viewing all of those tasks, mixed together, on the Timeline view can be confusing at best, or overwhelming. One suggestion is to categorize all your tasks. We discuss categorization in detail in Chapter 4. You can then group the Task Timeline view by category, and if you create a category for "Projects," for example, you can more easily view all your project tasks together.

Chapter 11

Reports

- Basic reports
- Working with reports
- Customizing a report

Basic reports

Reports are a great tool to help you manage your business. Reports, unlike views within a database, can be printed and shared with anyone at your organization, even people who are not users in your Business Contact Manager database. Business Contact Manager has over 50 reports to help you analyze and view the status of your accounts, business contacts, leads, opportunities, activities, business projects, and marketing campaigns. And customizing the reports is simple and straightforward, so you can run the reports that will provide you with relevant data.

Task A   Running an account report

Account reports provide a snapshot of your Business Contact Manager accounts, showing information about the accounts in a number of different ways. You can run an account report by category, such as customers and prospects, by the user assigned to an account, by territory, or by the source of lead for that account, and more.

To run an account report:

1. Click Business Contact Manager | Reports | Accounts. Choose the account report you would like to run. For this example, we will use the Quick Account List.
2. The report preview will appear, and you can print or save the report.
3. Click File | Close.

Account reports include:
- Accounts by City
- Accounts by State/Province
- Accounts by ZIP/Postal Code
- Accounts by Category
- Accounts by Rating
- Accounts by Payment Status
- Accounts by Assigned To
- Accounts by Territory
- Accounts by Source of Lead
- Account Activity Summary
- Quick Accounts List
- Neglected Accounts

Task B   Running a business contact report

Business contact reports provide a snapshot of your Business Contact Manager business contacts, showing you information about the business contacts in several ways. You can run a business contact report by category, such as customers and prospects, by the user assigned to a business contact, or by the source of lead for that business contact, and there is even a report that will show you your neglected business contacts.

To run a business contact report:

1. Click Business Contact Manager | Reports | Business Contacts. Choose the Business contact report you would like to run. For this example, we will use the Quick Business Contacts List.
2. The report preview will appear, and you can print or save the report.
3. Click File | Close.

Business contact reports include:
- Business Contacts by Account
- Business Contacts by Assigned To
- Business Contacts by City
- Business Contacts by State/Province
- Business Contacts by ZIP/Postal Code
- Business Contacts by Category
- Business Contacts by Rating
- Business Contacts by Payment Status
- Business Contacts by Source of Lead
- Business Contacts by Anniversary
- Business Contacts by Birthday
- Business Contact Activity Summary
- Quick Business Contacts List
- Neglected Business Contacts

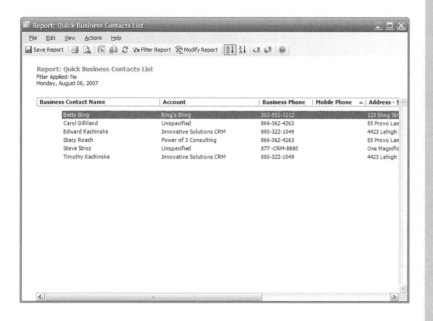

Lead reports include:
- Leads by Assigned To
- Leads by Assigned To and Rating
- Leads by Rating

Task C   Running a lead report

Leads are often the lifeblood of your business, so managing and tracking leads is a critical task. The Business Contact Manager lead reports provide a snapshot of your Business Contact Manager leads so that you can make sure that those leads are being followed up and managed effectively.

To run a lead report:

1. Click Business Contact Manager | Reports | Leads. Choose the Lead report you would like to run. For this example, we will use Leads by Rating.
2. The report preview will appear, and you can print or save the report.
3. Click File | Close.

Task D   Running an opportunity report

Chances are your business has customers that pay you money for products and services, in which case getting new customers as well as additional business from existing customers is probably one of the most critical functions for your organization. Opportunity reports are an important part of managing your sales process and pipeline. The Business Contact Manager opportunity reports provide a snapshot of your sales opportunities so you can make sure that those opportunities are being managed effectively.

To run an opportunity report:

1. Click Business Contact Manager | Reports | Opportunities. Choose the Opportunity report you would like to run. For this example we will use the Opportunity Forecast.
2. The report preview appears; you can print or save the report.
3. Click File | Close.

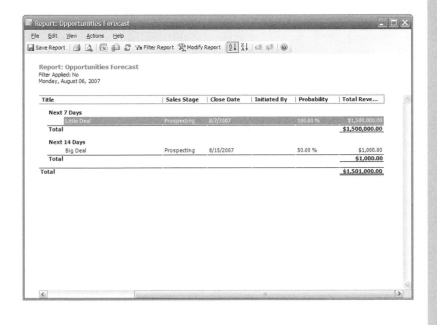

Opportunity reports include:

■ Opportunities by Account

■ Opportunities by Business Contact

■ Opportunities by Assigned To

■ Opportunities by Source of Lead

■ Opportunities by Product or Service Item

■ Opportunities Funnel

■ Past Due Opportunities

■ Opportunity Forecast

Task E   Running an activity report

Business contact reports provide a snapshot of your Business Contact Manager activities, showing you information about the activities in your Business Contact Manager database by business contact, account, or opportunity.

Activity reports include:

■ Activity by Business Contact
■ Activity by Account
■ Activity by Opportunity

To run an activity report:

1. Click Business Contact Manager | Reports | Activity. Choose the activity report you would like to run. For this example, we will use the Activity by Opportunity report.
2. The report preview appears; you can print or save the report.
3. Click File | Close.

Task F Running a business project report

Effectively managing projects is an important part of most organizations. Business project reports provide a snapshot of your business projects, showing you information about the business projects in your Business Contact Manager database in a number of different ways. You can run a business project report by due date, by the user assigned to a business project, or by the priority of a business project. You can also run reports on your projects tasks.

To run a business project report:

1. Click Business Contact Manager | Reports | Business Projects. Choose the business project report you would like to run. For this example, we will use the Business Projects by Due Date report.
2. The report preview appears; you can print or save the report.
3. Click File | Close.

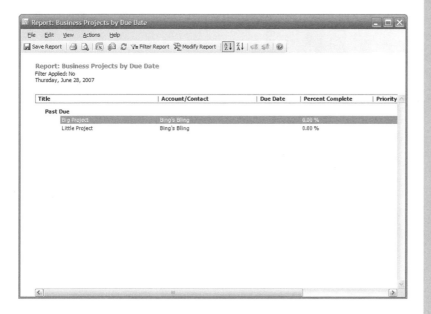

Business project reports include:

- Business Projects by Status
- Business Projects by Due Date
- Business Projects by Assigned To
- Business Projects by Type
- Business Projects by Priority
- Business Projects by Account
- Business Projects by Business Contact
- Quick Business Projects List
- Project Tasks per Project
- Project Tasks by Assigned To

Marketing campaign reports include:

■ Opportunities by Marketing
  Campaign
■ Business Contacts by Marketing
  Campaign
■ Accounts by Marketing Campaign

Task G | **Running a marketing campaign report**

Investing in marketing is a smart business decision, provided that the investment pays off. Marketing campaign reports in Business Contact Manager
provide a snapshot of your marketing campaigns, showing you information
about the marketing campaigns in your Business Contact Manager database in
a number of different ways.

To run a marketing campaign report:

1. Click Business Contact Manager | Reports | Marketing Campaigns.
    Choose the marketing campaign report you would like to run. For this
    example, we will use the Business Contacts by Marketing Campaign
    report.
2. The report preview appears; you can print or save the report.
3. Click File | Close.

Working with reports

Once you have determined which report or reports best suit your particular needs, you can refresh the report data, save the report, filter the report to only show some information, export a report to Microsoft Excel for further analysis, or even e-mail a report as an Excel attachment.

Task A Refreshing a report

Reports tend to be snapshots in time, but you can always refresh a report in the preview mode to make sure that you are viewing the most up-to-the-minute information.

To refresh a report:

1. For this example, we will use the Opportunity Forecast report. Click Business Contact Manager | Reports | Opportunities. Choose the Opportunity Forecast report.
2. The report preview appears. To refresh the report, click View | Refresh Report or press the F5 key on your keyboard.
3. You can print or save the report.
4. Click File | Close.

Task B   Running a saved report

If you customize a report, you can save that report and run it repeatedly. The way to access your customized reports is to open a saved report.

Remember, if you are opening a saved report, and you want to view the most current data, you should refresh the report. You can refresh by clicking View | Refresh Report. Of course, if the saved report was a snapshot in time that you want to preserve, you would not refresh the report.

To run a saved report:

1. Click Business Contact Manager | Reports | Open Saved Report.
2. Select the saved report you want to open and click Open.
3. The report preview appears; you can print or save the report.
4. Click File | Close.

Task C   Filtering a report

Reports are a great way to view and analyze important information pertaining to your business. If you have to wade through a bunch of irrelevant data in a report, then that report has lost its value. You can use the powerful filtering options in Business Contact Manager reports to show just the information that you want or need to see on a given report.

To filter a report:

1. For this task, we will be running the Opportunity Forecast report. Click Business Contact Manager | Reports | Opportunities. Choose the Opportunity Forecast report.
2. The report preview appears. To filter the report, click Actions | Filter Report or press Ctrl + F on your keyboard.
3. This will open the Filter dialog box. On the Simple Filter tab, select the filters you would like to apply. The filter options will depend on the report you are running.
4. Click the Advanced Filter tab and you can create multiple criteria to filter the report.
5. On the Review Results you can preview what data will appear on the report after the filtering options are applied.
6. Click OK and the report will be updated to reflect the filtering options you selected. Note that at the top of the report, under the report title, the Filter Applied indication will be Yes.
7. You can print or save the report.
8. Click File | Close.

You have several filtering options in Business Contact Manager reports. When you access the Filter dialog box in a report, the Simple Filter tab will show you a variety of filtering options that you can select with the click of a mouse. The Advanced Filter allows you to further refine the report filters and combine multiple filters to really hone in on just the data you want to see in a report. The Review Results tab will let you see a preview of the data that will be included in the report once you apply the filters, so that if there is an issue with any of your filters, you have a chance to tweak them before applying the filters to the report.

Task D   Exporting a report to Excel

Business Contact Manager provides quite a few options for analyzing and refining your reports right in the report preview. If you need more analysis horsepower, you can always export the report to Microsoft Excel and take advantage of the multitude of analysis possibilities available to you in Excel. Pivot tables, anyone?

If you start running reports and then constantly re-run them to get updated information, you might consider customizing a view of the Business Contact Manager dashboard instead. The dashboard provides updated information right on the dashboard view. And you can save some paper!

To export a report to Excel:

1. For this task, we will run the Opportunity Forecast report. Click Business Contact Manager | Reports | Opportunities. Choose the Opportunity Forecast report.

2. The report preview appears; click File | Export to Excel.

3. The report will export to Excel, and Excel will open with the report displayed. For reports with a lot of data, this export may take some time.

4. In Excel you can now manipulate and analyze the data, as well as print and save the Excel version of the report.

5. Click on the Microsoft button and click Close. You will be back in the Business Contact Manager preview of the report.

6. You can print or save the report.

7. Click File | Close.

Task E — E-mailing a report as an Excel attachment

Reports are an excellent tool to share the important information about your business. And sharing a sales forecast report is a frequent requirement for most organizations. Business Contact Manager reports make it easy to run a report and e-mail that report to others in your organization as an Excel attachment.

To e-mail a report as an Excel attachment:

1. For this task we will be running the Opportunity Forecast report. Click Business Contact Manager | Reports | Opportunities. Choose the Opportunity Forecast report.
2. The report preview appears; click File | Send E-mail with Excel Attachment.
3. Address the e-mail message and send as you would normally. Note that the report in Excel format is already attached to the e-mail message.
4. You can then print or save the report.
5. Click File | Close.

When you e-mail a report as an Excel attachment, you won't get to preview how the report looks in Excel before you send the e-mail message. If you want to take a look at the report first and make any changes, you can export the report to Excel and then send that Excel file as an attachment to an e-mail. We cover the steps to export a report to Excel in Task D.

Customizing a report

Business Contact Manager has 50 default reports, which is a great start. But the real power of the Business Contact Manager reports is evident in the ease with which you can customize those reports to more accurately reflect your unique business model and sales process.

Task A   Adding a field to an existing report

Adding a field to an existing report is accomplished with just a few clicks of your mouse. You can select from basic fields related to that report, as well as tracking fields, which include things like who created/modified the data and when the data was created/modified.

To add a field to an existing report:

1. For this task we will be modifying the Opportunity Forecast report. Click Business Contact Manager | Reports | Opportunities. Choose the Opportunity Forecast report.
2. The report preview appears, click View | Modify Report Pane, or click the Modify Report icon on the toolbar.
3. The Modify Report pane appears on the right-hand side of the report preview.
4. Under the Columns section, click the plus sign (+) in front of Basic Columns and check the box for any fields you want to add to this report. For this example, we will add Expected Revenue. Notice that the new column appears all the way on the right-hand side of the report preview.
5. You can close the Modify Report pane by clicking on the X in the top-right corner of the pane.
6. To run this report with your changes again, be sure to save the report.
7. Click File | Close.

Business Contact Manager report customizations can be applied to the following elements of a report:

- Filters—the data you see on a report
- Columns—which columns of data appear on your report
- Fonts and Numbers—the format and style of the text in the report
- Header and Footer—the information displayed at the top and bottom of each page of the report

Task B Removing a field from an existing report

Customizing a report is a great way to make sure that the information displayed on any given report is valuable and applicable to your organization. If there are fields or data that are not applicable to your organization, you can remove those columns from the report with a couple of quick mouse clicks.

To remove a field from an existing report:

1. For this task we will modify the Opportunity Forecast report. Click Business Contact Manager | Reports | Opportunities. Choose the Opportunity Forecast report.

2. The report preview appears; click View | Modify Report Pane, or press the Ctrl + M keys on your keyboard.

3. The Modify Report pane appears on the right-hand side of the report preview.

4. Under the Columns section, click the plus sign (+) in front of Basic Columns and uncheck the box for any fields you want to remove from this report. For this example, we will remove the column for Initiated By. Simply click the check box for Initiated By to clear the check mark in that box. Notice that the field you unchecked disappears immediately from the report preview.

5. You can close the Modify Report pane by clicking on the X in the top-right corner of the pane.

6. To run this report with these modifications again in the future, be sure to save the report.

7. Click File | Close.

When you are moving columns of data around in your report, you might not always get the order exactly right. There is no undo function after you move a column in the report preview, so you can just close the report without saving, rerun the report, and then move the columns to the desired location.

Task C   Changing the order of columns in an existing report

Once you have added and/or removed columns from your report, you may want to change the order of the columns on the report. The layout of a report can be modified easily and columns of data can be quickly moved around through the click and drag function right in the report preview.

To change the order of columns in an existing report:

1. For this task we will modify the Business Projects by Due Date report. Click Business Contact Manager | Reports | Business Projects | Business Projects by Due Date.

2. The report preview will appear. We will be moving the Status column, which is on the far-right column, between the Account/Contact and Due Date column.

3. Simply left-click on the Status column header and drag to the location where you would like that column to appear. Notice the vertical blue line that appears; this shows you where the column will be when you release the left mouse button.

4. To run this report with your changes again, be sure to save the report.

5. Click File | Close.

Task D Changing the sort order of an existing report

Like many common report functions, changing the sort order of a report is very easy in Business Contact Manager. You can quickly sort your report by any of the column headers in that report with a simple mouse click on the column header.

To change the sort order of an existing report:

1. For this task we will modify the Quick Business Projects List report. Click Business Contact Manager | Reports | Business Projects | Quick Business Projects report.
2. The report preview appears. To change the sort order of the report, simply click on one of the column headers. For this example, we will use the Due Date report. Notice that the report re-sorts immediately right in the report preview. A gray triangle appears in the column header next to the column that the report is now sorted by.
3. When we clicked on the Due Date column header, we sorted the report by Due Date, ascending. You can sort by that same column, descending, just by clicking on the column header again. Click the same column one last time, and the sort on that column is removed.
4. To run this report with your changes again, be sure to save the report.
5. Click File | Close.

When you make any changes to a report, from adding a column to changing the sort order of the report to adding your company's name to the header of a report, those changes are reflected immediately in the report preview, making it easy to spot any issues or problems before you print, e-mail, or save that report.

If you have customized, filtered, and/or changed the sort order of a report, you can use the Notes area to communicate these changes right on the report. That way, if you look back at the report, or are reviewing the data on a report with other folks in your organization, you can see right on the report itself the changes that you made for that report. The notes for a report are displayed in the report header, right under the date the report was created.

Task E   Modifying the header and footer on an existing report

The information in a report header appears at the top of each page of a report. The information in the report footer appears at the bottom of each page of a report. Whether you are running one of the stock Business Contact Manager reports or e-mailing a highly customized report, you will probably want to edit the information that appears in the header and/or footer. You can add your company name, company URL, the title and subtitle of the report, the filters applied to the report, the date the report was created, and any notes about the report.

To modify the header and footer on an existing report:

1. For this task we will modify the Opportunity Forecast report. Click Business Contact Manager | Reports | Opportunities. Choose the Opportunity Forecast report.
2. The report preview appears. Click View | Modify Report Pane, or press the Ctrl + M keys on your keyboard.
3. The Modify Report pane appears on the right-hand side of the report preview.
4. Under the Modify Report section, click Header and Footer. The Header and Footer section appears.
5. To include any of the data elements listed under the Header and Footer section, simply click the check box for that element. For this example, we will be adding your company name to the report header.
6. Click the Company Name check box, and in the box below, highlight the words "Company Name" and type your company name instead. Notice that your company name appears immediately on the report preview, as you type.
7. To run this report with your changes again, be sure to save the report.
8. Click File | Close.

Chapter 12

Creating a Dashboard

- Viewing your dashboards
- Customizing your dashboard

Viewing your dashboards

Business Contact Manager has a very powerful and functional element—the dashboard. The dashboard in your car is designed to give you up to the minute information that will help you drive; the Business Contact Manager dashboard provides the same kind of immediate view into important elements that you can use to better manage your business. The dashboard view is also easily customized and filtered to select only the most relevant data specific to your business model and/or sales process. In addition, the dashboard contains short cuts to important functions, like running reports and creating new marketing campaigns, business projects, and business tasks.

Task A   Viewing the standard dashboard

Dashboards take all the critical data and information in your Business Contact Manager database and present that data in a way that facilitates quick evaluation of the key indicators for your business. Want to see the current Opportunity Funnel Chart as well as track the status of critical business projects? Just go to the Business Contact Manager dashboard.

To view the standard dashboard:

1. From anywhere in Outlook, click the Business Contact Manager Home button on the toolbar.
2. Alternatively, you can click Business Contact Manager | Business Contact Manager Home or press Alt + M.
3. The Business Contact Manager Home screen should appear. There are four standard tabs in this dashboard view: Home, Sales, Marketing, and Projects. Click on each tab to see the default data in each view.

The dashboard is just like the one in your car; you know, the one that has all the dials and gauges, the one that tells you how fast you're going, how much gas you have left, and even if your engine needs service. The dashboard in Business Contact Manager provides the same kind of information. Because it pulls the data from your Business Contact Manager database, you will be able to quickly review relevant and time-sensitive information to help you manage your business and make critical business decisions.

Task B   Navigating the dashboard sections

The dashboard is designed to visually present the information in your Business Contact Manager database in a way that allows you to quickly view the most important data, and then make informed business decisions. Navigating the dashboard is simple and straightforward—most of the navigation is simply clicking through the dashboard tabs.

To navigate the dashboard sections:

1. To get to the Business Contact Manager Home screen, or dashboard view, click Business Contact Manager | Business Contact Manager Home or press Alt +M.

2. You will now be viewing the Business Contact Manager or dashboard view. There are four standard tabs in the dashboard view: Home, Sales, Marketing, and Project. Each tab on the dashboard has several sections, which can be hidden or closed.

3. The default first area on each tab is the Online Spotlight. This section provides links to online information you can view under the Learn section, such as "How to grow with your business" and tools you can purchase under the Buy section, such as "Purchase Leads."

4. The second area on each tab is the Start a Task section. You can quickly initiate different tasks in your Business Contact Manager database by clicking on a task in this section from the Sales, Marketing, or Projects tabs. On the Home tab, clicking any of the Start a Task options simply opens the view you clicked on. For example, on the Home tab of the Business Contact Manager dashboard, clicking on the Opportunities bar in the Start a Task section will take you to the Opportunity view in Business Contact Manager.

5. The next area on each tab is the Reports section. This section provides you the ability to quickly run a report.

6. The last area is a details section for the tab you are on. On the Projects tab, for example, you will see a list of open business projects. On the Marketing tab, you will see a list of marketing campaigns.

You can customize your dashboard view to display just the information that you want to see, and if you have a shared database, each user can have her own dashboard view.

These are the sections you can add to the Business Contact Manager dashboard:

- Online Spotlight
- Start a Task
- Reports
- Opportunity Funnel Chart
- Open Opportunities
- Opportunity Pipeline Chart
- Opportunity Summary by Source Chart
- Opportunity Summary by Assigned Chart
- Opportunity Summary by Initiated By Chart
- Business Contacts with Excellent Rating
- Business Contact Recent History
- Account Recent History
- Opportunity Recent History
- Business Project Recent History
- Open Business Projects
- Open Project Tasks
- Marketing Campaigns
- Business Leads
- Deals closing in next 7 days
- Prospects
- Current Open Projects

Customizing your dashboard

The default Business Contact Manager dashboard views are very good, but you can make the dashboard view even more powerful by customizing the views to more closely map to your business model and/or sales process. You can quickly and easily add and remove sections from the dashboard, hide sections on the dashboard, change the order of the sections, and add fields to the dashboard views.

Task A   Adding a dashboard section

Adding relevant content to the dashboard is one of the best things you do can to boost the functionality of the dashboard view. Adding a section to a dashboard view is as easy as clicking a check box.

To add a new dashboard section:

1. To get to the Business Contact Manager Home screen, or dashboard view, click Business Contact Manager | Business Contact Manager Home or press Alt +M.
2. You will now be viewing the Business Contact Manager Home or dashboard view. Select a tab to customize. For this example, we will add a section to the Home tab.
3. Click the Add or Remove Content link in the top-right corner of the Business Contact Manager view.
4. To add content selections, simply click the check box in front of that selection. In this example, we will add Deals closing in the next 7 days.
5. Click OK to close the Add or Remove Content dialog box. You will now be viewing the new content on your dashboard.

Task B   Hiding dashboard sections

Viewing timely and relevant business data is the whole point of an effective dashboard. Having to wade through or ignore irrelevant content is inefficient. Luckily Business Contact Manager makes it easy to temporarily hide sections of the dashboard so that you can zero in on the most important pieces of information at any given time.

To hide a dashboard section:

1. To get to the Business Contact Manager Home screen, or dashboard view, click Business Contact Manager | Business Contact Manager Home or press Alt +M.
2. You will now be viewing the Business Contact Manager or dashboard view. Select a tab on which you would like to hide a dashboard section. For this example, we will hide a section on the Home tab.
3. On the top right of blue title bar of the section, the chevron (⌃)pointing up indicates that that section is visible. To hide a section, simply click the chevron and it will point down. For this task, hide the Start a Task section.
4. The blue title bar of the task remains visible, but the content of that section is hidden.

Task C Removing existing dashboard sections

Honing in on the key indicators for your business and adding the appropriate sections to your dashboard view is a great start, but don't forget that you can remove sections of the dashboard view that are not applicable to your organization's use of Business Contact Manager.

If you find yourself hiding the same section of a dashboard view repeatedly, you might want to consider removing that section from the view. You can always add it back later if you need it.

To remove existing dashboard sections:

1. To get to the Business Contact Manager Home screen, or dashboard view, click Business Contact Manager | Business Contact Manager Home or press Alt +M.
2. You will now be viewing the Business Contact Manager or dashboard view. Select a tab on which you would like to remove a dashboard section. For this example, we will remove a section on the Projects tab.
3. Click on the Projects tab and then click Add or Remove Content.
4. In the list of content section, find the section you want to remove. We will remove the Online Spotlight section, since it appears on each tab.
5. Simply remove the check mark in front of the section titled Online Spotlight, then click OK.
6. You can also remove content right from the dashboard view. Click on the Marketing tab, and on the top right of the blue title bar for the Online Spotlight section, click the X.

Task D   Customizing fields shown on a dashboard section

Your business is unique, and your dashboard can reflect that. You can customize any of the list views in the dashboard view to add/remove fields from your Business Contact Manager database, thus ensuring that you are viewing the most pertinent data in your all-important dashboard view.

To customize fields shown on a dashboard section:

1. To get to the Business Contact Manager Home screen, or dashboard view, click Business Contact Manager | Business Contact Manager Home or press Alt +M.

2. You will now be viewing the Business Contact Manager Home or dashboard view. Select a tab on which you would like customize the fields shown in that dashboard section. For this example, we will remove a section on the Projects tab.

3. Click View | Current View | Customize Current View. The Customize View dialog box will open, and it will indicate at the top the name of the view you are customizing. In this case it will say [Business Projects List].

4. Click Fields. This brings up the Show Fields dialog box. Click in the Select available fields from drop-down and select User-defined fields in folder.

5. In the list of Available fields on the left, select the field to add, and select Project Type.

6. Click the Add button to move that field to the Show these fields in this order list.

7. To change the order, simply click on a field in the Show these fields in this order list and click the Move Up or Move Down buttons.

8. Click OK. You will now see the fields you added to this view.

You can add your own custom fields to the dashboard view as well, which is one of the best ways to make sure that the data on the dashboard is relevant to your business model and/or sales process.

| Task E | **Changing the order of sections on your dashboard** |

Shifting the sections of your dashboard view is easy, and it is a great way to make sure that the most important and relevant content is front and center in your dashboard view.

To change the order of sections on your dashboard:

1. To get to the Business Contact Manager Home screen, or dashboard view, click Business Contact Manager | Business Contact Manager Home or press Alt +M.

2. You will now be viewing the Business Contact Manager or dashboard view. Select a tab on which you would like to remove a dashboard section. For this example, we will add the graph of the Opportunity Funnel and move that to the top of the Sales tab.

3. Click on the Sales tab and then click Add or Remove Content.

4. Click the Opportunity Funnel Chart check box.

5. Click the Move Up button on the right until the Opportunity Funnel Chart is at the top of the list.

6. Click OK. Your sales dashboard will now have the graph of the Opportunity Funnel Chart at the top.

Once you start adding new content to your dashboard, you will quickly realize that the value of the dashboard is wholly dependent on the data in your Business Contact Manager database. If you don't enter the information, you won't be able to see it in the dashboard.

Task F   Automatically open Outlook 2007 in the dashboard view

The dashboard view is so powerful and useful that you might just want to have that view displayed automatically when you start Outlook. By setting Outlook to open to the Business Contact Manager folder, the dashboard view will be the first thing that you look at every day.

To automatically open Outlook 2007 in the dashboard view:

1. In Outlook, click Tools | Options, then click the Other tab.
2. In the General section, click Advanced Options.
3. In the General settings section, in the Startup in this folder selection, click the Browse button.
4. You will now be viewing all of your Outlook folders. Click on the Business Contact Manager folder and click OK three times.
5. Now close and reopen Outlook. Your starting view will be the Business Contact Manager dashboard.

You can quickly and easily set Outlook to automatically display the Business Contact Manager dashboard view whenever you open Outlook. That way, you are able to start every day with the most important data for your business prominently displayed.

Chapter 13

Customizing Your Database

- Adding new fields to forms
- Modifying placement of custom fields
- Managing drop-down fields

Adding new fields to forms

You can create up to 40 user-defined fields for any type of database entity. So, you could have 40 custom fields for contacts, 40 for opportunities, 40 for accounts, etc. Adding new fields to a database only takes a few clicks, and any user in the master database can do it.

Task A   Adding custom fields

You may want to categorize your contacts. Perhaps you want to specify whether a business contact or contact has established terms? Maybe you want to track whether an opportunity is a referral from an existing customer? You can add custom fields to track information for your business contacts, accounts, opportunities, and more.

Types of fields that can be added to a Business Contact Manager database are as follows:

- Text
- Number
- Percent
- Currency
- Yes/No
- Date/Time
- Integer
- Drop-down list

Field names can only be 64 characters long and cannot include any of the following characters: [,],-, or #.

To add a custom field to the database:

1. Click Business Contact Manager | Customize Forms | Manage User-Defined Fields and choose whether you want to add an account, business contact, opportunity, or business project field.
2. Click the Add Field button.
3. Choose the option to add a new field.
4. Type a field name in the Field name field.
5. In the Data type drop-down, select the type of field you'd like to add.
6. Click OK twice to return to Business Contact Manager.

Task B Adding a user-defined field that has already been created

Let's say you have an account field called Hot Prospect. You also want to have a business contact field called Hot Prospect. If you try to add it, you'll get an error—because the field called Hot Prospect already exists in the accounts table. You can reuse field names across tables by following the steps in this task.

To add a user-defined field that has already been created in another table:

1. Click Business Contact Manager | Customize Forms | Manage User-Defined Fields and choose whether you want to add an account, business contact, opportunity, or business project field.
2. Click the Add Field button.
3. Choose the option to add a user-defined field that has already been created.
4. Choose a field from the list.
5. Click OK twice to save changes and return to Business Contact Manager.

Text fields can only contain up to 96 characters.

181

Modifying placement of custom fields

After adding fields to a database, you'll need to figure out where to put them on the form. You can add them to the main page within any form, or you can add a custom field in the User-Defined Fields page. These instructions apply to accounts, business contacts, opportunities, and business projects.

Task A   Adding new groups of fields

Within the left and right columns of any page on a form, you can add groups of fields. Keeping your fields separated by groups helps visually sort them and can make it easier for you to find fields related to a broader topic.

To add a new group of fields on a form:

1. Click Business Contact Manager | Customize Forms | Manage User-Defined Fields and choose whether you want to customize the account, business contact, opportunity, or business project field form
2. From the Page drop-down, select the page of the form you'd like to edit.
3. Click the Add Group button.
4. Type the name of your group and click OK.
5. Your group will appear somewhere on the page. Highlight it and click the Move To, Move Up, Move Down, <<, or >> buttons to move the placement of the group.
6. Click OK to save your changes.

Once you have a group defined, you can move fields into the group. See the next page for instructions.

Task B Moving a field on a form

The account, business contact, opportunity, and business project forms are all divided into four pages: User-Defined Fields, General, Details, and History. Most of these pages are divided into two columns, and you can place fields in either column. Not surprisingly, the columns are referred to in Business Contact Manager as the left column and the right column.

To move a field on a form:

1. Click Business Contact Manager | Customize Forms | Manage User-Defined Fields and choose whether you want to customize the placement of an account, business contact, opportunity, or business project field.
2. In the Page drop-down, select the page that contains the user-defined field you'd like to move.
3. Highlight the field you'd like to move.
4. Click the Move To button to move the field to another page.
5. Click the Move Up and Move Down buttons to move the placement of the field up or down.
5. Click the >> or << buttons to move a field from one column to another.
6. Click OK to save your changes.

To delete a field, click the field in the Manage User-Defined Fields dialog box and click the Delete button. Be careful, though. Short of restoring a backup, there is no way to easily undo a field deletion.

Business Project - Manage User-Defined Fields

Click the Page box to select a page. Add, edit, or move groups or fields in the selected page's Left Column and Right Column.

Page: User-Defined Fields

Left Column

New Group 1

Add Group...
Add Field...
Edit...
Delete
Move To...
Move Up
Move Down
<<
>>

Right Column

New Group 2
　Begin Date
New Group 1
　Second Field

Help   OK   Cancel

Managing drop-down fields

Keeping information in drop-down fields can greatly increase the consistency of the data entered into your database. Instead of having to come up with a unique value for a field each time a new contact, account, or opportunity is entered, a drop-down field forces the user to choose a value from a pre-defined list of items.

Task A Creating a new drop-down list

The only way to create a drop-down list is to add a new drop-down field to the database. One of the field types available in Business Contact Manager is Drop-down list, and when you add a field of this type, a drop-down list is automatically created and linked with the field.

To create a new drop-down list:

The drop-down list is automatically created when you add a drop-down field to the database. You cannot create a drop-down list independently of a drop-down field.

1. Click Business Contact Manager | Customize Forms | Manage User-Defined Fields and choose whether you want to add an account, business contact, opportunity, or business project field.
2. Click the Add Field button.
3. Choose the option to add a new field.
4. Type a name in the Field name field.
5. In the Data type drop-down, choose Drop-down list.
6. Click OK twice to return to Business Contact Manager.

Task B   Editing items in an existing drop-down list

As your business needs change, you may need to add, remove, or modify items in the drop-down lists on your fields. You can use this procedure to edit drop-down lists on both core fields and user-defined fields.

To edit an existing drop-down:

1. Click Business Contact Manager | Customize Forms | Edit Lists.
2. From the Selected list drop-down, choose the drop-down list you'd like to edit.
3. Click the Add button to add a new item to the list.
4. Highlight any item and click Rename to change the item's name.
5. Click the Delete or Replace button to delete an item.
6. Click OK to save your changes.

If you delete an item in a drop-down, any record that currently has that value in the field will be reverted to a blank value for the field.

Chapter 14

Offline Databases

■ Creating an offline database

Creating an offline database

If you need remote access to a Business Contact Manager database, you can configure the database for offline use. Some other programs refer to this feature as remote synchronization. Offline databases in Business Contact Manager work much the same way offline folders work with Windows networking.

Task A Setting Business Contact Manager to work offline

Before you can follow the steps in this task, the following conditions must be true:

- You must have created a database on a computer that will act as your server.
- You must have granted the remote user access to this computer.
- You must have the server database open from the remote computer.
- Your server and workstation must be connected on the same local network.

To set up your remote database to work offline:

1. Open the server database from your remote computer. The remote computer should be on the same local area network as the server computer while you perform this task.
2. Click Business Contact Manager | Offline | Enable/Disable Offline.
3. Choose Yes to use Business Contact Manager on this computer while you are away from the office.
4. Click the Offline Settings option.
5. Choose how often you would like to synchronize data between the shared and local database.
6. Click the Conflict Resolution tab and choose what to do if data has been changed on both the offline and online database between synchronizations.
7. Click OK twice to create the offline database and set your computer to work in offline mode when not connected.

Unless you select otherwise in the Offline Settings dialog box, Business Contact Manager will automatically switch you back to using the server database whenever the computer is connected to the network with access to the Business Contact Manager server.

Task B Using the offline database while connected to the LAN or VPN

After enabling offline database use, you can manually select whether to use the server or offline database. You might do this if you are connected to a VPN in an area where your connection is slow or intermittent. In such a case, you could force Business Contact Manager to always use your offline database, which will be faster and more reliable than the server database.

To force Business Contact Manager to work offline:

1. Click Business Contact Manager | Offline | Work Offline. (This option is only available if you are actually connected to the network that houses the Business Contact Manager server.)
2. Business Contact Manager will be set to work offline, even though you have LAN or VPN access to your server.

Once you click the Work Offline option on the Business Contact Manager | Offline menu, you'll see a check mark next to the option. Click Business Contact Manager | Offline | Work Offline to uncheck this option and return to using the server database directly whenever it is available.

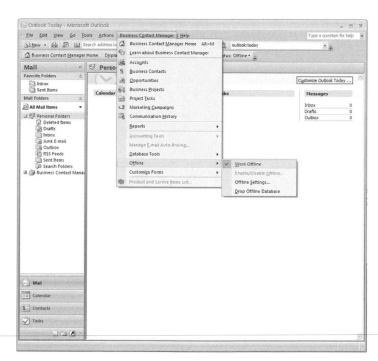

Task C Configuring offline database settings

After you have created an offline database, you can go back and reset the offline database settings to set how often information is synchronized with the server, how Business Contact Manager switches between the server and offline database, and how the program handles data conflicts.

To configure offline database settings:

1. Click Business Contact Manager | Offline | Offline Settings.
2. Select how often you would like to synchronize data between the shared and local database.
3. Choose whether you'd like to automatically switch between the local and shared database when the shared database is available.
4. Click the Conflict Resolution tab. Choose what to do when there is a data conflict.
5. Click OK.

Task D Dropping an offline database

If you decide that you no longer need to use your shared database offline, you can drop the offline database. It's a good idea to make sure your offline and shared databases are in sync before dropping the offline version.

To drop an offline database:

1. Click Business Contact Manager | Offline | Drop Offline Database.
2. Click Yes to confirm that you would like to drop the offline database.
3. Click the export option if you would like to make a backup of your offline database before dropping it.
4. If you chose to export, specify a file name for the export and click Next twice.
5. Click Close.

Why drop an offline database? When you choose to use a database offline, a copy of the database is actually made on your local computer. That copy takes up space on your computer, and if you no longer need it, you can drop the offline database.

After dropping the offline database, you will still be able to use your shared database; you just won't be able to use it in offline mode.

Chapter 15

Database Maintenance

- Import and export
- Sending data between Outlook and Business Contact Manager
- Backup and restore
- Database maintenance

Import and export

It's easy to get your data into and out of Business Contact Manager. The import wizard lets you import text files, ACT! databases, Excel spreadsheets, and more. Need to get your data out of Business Contact Manager? With a few clicks, you can get a text file or Excel spreadsheet of your business contacts or accounts.

Task A Importing a data file

Let's say you get a spreadsheet of contacts that you'd like to incorporate into your Business Contact Manager database. Or maybe you just want to import some contacts from another program. Business Contact Manager makes it easy to import an existing data file into your business contact list.

Types of files you can import:
- Business Contact Manager data
- CSV text files
- Access databases
- Excel Workbooks
- Outlook contacts
- Microsoft sales leads
- ACT! databases
- Quickbooks

To import a data file (like a text file) into Business Contact Manager:

1. Click File | Import and Export | Business Contact Manager for Outlook.
2. The Business Data Import and Export wizard appears.
3. Select Import a file and click Next.
4. Choose the type of file you'd like to import and click Next.
5. Click the Browse button, and double-click the file you'd like to import.
6. Select whether to import duplicates and click Next.
7. In the Import data section, choose the files you'd like to import and click the Map button to create a data map. Once you've set the map, click Next.
8. A confirmation screen appears. Click Next.
9. Click Close and verify within your database that the imported data is correct.

Task B Converting ACT! or QuickBooks databases

If you have made the switch from ACT! to Business Contact Manager, or if you'd like to bring in all of your clients from QuickBooks, you can convert that data to Business Contact Manager format and then import it into your business contacts list.

To convert an ACT! or QuickBooks database into Business Contact Manager:

1. Click File | Import and Export | Business Contact Manager for Outlook.
2. The Business Data Import and Export wizard appears.
3. Select Import a file and click Next.
4. Choose the ACT! (or QuickBooks) option and click Next. Choosing either option will bring you to the same conversion wizard.
5. Click the Convert Data option.
6. The Data Conversion Tool dialog box appears. Click Next.
7. Select your version of ACT! or QuickBooks and click Next.
8. Follow the on-screen instructions to convert your ACT! or QuickBooks data to Business Contact Manager format. Once the data is in Business Contact Manager format, you will be able to import it into your existing database. See the previous task for instructions on importing into your database.

Compatible versions for conversion:
- ACT! 2005
- ACT! 4.0-6.0
- QuickBooks 1999-2005

Data Conversion Tool

Convert

Select the program from which you want to convert data into Business Contact Manager file format.

Applications

ACT! 2005/7.0 (.pad)
ACT! 4.0, 2000/5.0, 2003/6.0 (.dbf)
QuickBooks 99, 2000, 2001, 2002, 2003, 2004, 2005 (.IIF)

Help   < Back   Next >   Cancel

Task C   Exporting Business Contact Manager data to other formats

You can export a Business Contact Manager database to another Business Contact Manager database in addition to a text file. If you are trying to get data from Business Contact Manager into another database, exporting to a text file will make it easy to get your contacts and accounts into just about any database.

Types of export output formats:

- Business Contact Manager data
- Business Contact Manager customizations
- CSV text

If you are exporting to an Excel spreadsheet, try running a report instead. After running most reports, you can click File | Export to Excel to create a spreadsheet of the current report.

To export Business Contact Manager data to other formats:

1. Click File | Import and Export | Business Contact Manager for Outlook.
2. The Business Data Import and Export wizard appears.
3. Select Export a file and click Next.
4. Select a format for your output file and click Next.
5. Select whether you'd like to export business contacts or accounts.
6. If you want to specify a filter for the records that are exported, choose the bottom option. Click Next.
7. Specify a file name and location. Click Next.
8. Click Next to begin the export.

Task D   Exporting Business Contact Manager customization

Exporting Business Contact Manager customization will export data from the user-defined fields in the currently open Business Contact Manager database to a .bcmx file that can be imported into any other Business Contact Manager database.

To export Business Contact Manager customization:

1. Click File | Import and Export | Business Contact Manager for Outlook.
2. The Business Data Import and Export wizard appears.
3. Select Export a file and click Next.
4. Choose the Business Contact Manager Customizations (.bcmx) type and click Next.
5. Specify a file name and location. Click Next.
6. Click Next to begin the export.

Only the database owner or an administrator for the database host computer can import user-defined fields.

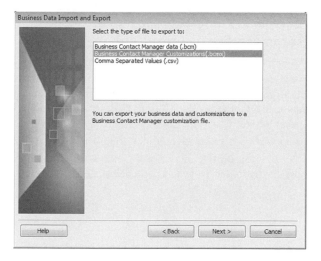

Sending data between Outlook and Business Contact Manager

A common misconception is that Business Contact Manager shares its contact list with Outlook. It does not. After installing Business Contact Manager, a separate database is created where Business Contact Manager data is stored. Business Contact Manager business contacts and accounts appear within the Outlook interface, but these business contacts are not the same as regular Outlook contacts. If you have an add-on product that interfaces with Outlook, it may not interface with Business Contact Manager.

Task A Copying Outlook contacts to Business Contact Manager

If you have an existing contact list in Outlook, you can bring your contacts into Business Contact Manager by dragging them from the Contacts folder to the Business Contacts folder.

Hold down the Ctrl key while you are dragging to make a copy of the Outlook contacts in Business Contact Manager. Simply dragging the contacts will move them, not copy them.

To move Outlook/Exchange contacts to the Business Contact Manager business contacts list:

1. Click Business Contact Manager | Business Contacts. This brings up a list of business contacts in Outlook.
2. On the left pane, locate the My Contacts header. Under this header, you should see a folder called Contacts. The Contacts folder is where all of your Outlook contacts are stored. Click the Contacts folder.
3. Highlight the contact or contacts you would like to move.
4. Drag the contacts to the Business Contacts in Business Contact Manager folder. You should see the folder in the left pane below the My Contacts group.

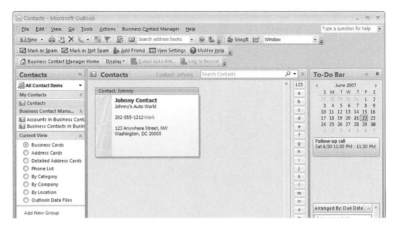

Task B Moving Business Contact Manager business contacts to Outlook

You can move Business Contact Manager business contacts into Outlook by simply dragging them to your Outlook contacts folder. If you have an add-on product that interfaces with Outlook but not with Business Contact Manager, you may need to move your Business Contact Manager contacts into Outlook.

To copy Business Contact Manager business contacts to Outlook:

1. Click Business Contact Manager | Business Contacts. This brings up a list of business contacts in Outlook.
2. Highlight the Business Contact Manager business contacts you would like to copy.
3. Drag the contact or contacts to the Contacts folder in the My Contacts group in the left pane of the Outlook interface.

When you drag from Business Contact Manager to Outlook, contacts are copied. When you drag from Outlook to Business Contact Manager, the contacts are moved.

Backup and restore

This section is perhaps the most important in this entire book. It doesn't matter what you do to your database, as long as you have a current backup. You should plan on backing up the Business Contact Manager database as often as you don't mind losing data. So, if you don't mind losing a day's worth of data, backup every day. If you don't mind re-keying a month of contacts, go ahead and backup once a month.

Task A   Backing up your Business Contact Manager database

Backing up your Business Contact Manager database will make a backup of all Business Contact Manager data tables, including extra database items like business notes and attached e-mail messages. Your Outlook contacts and Inbox/other e-mail folders are not included in a Business Contact Manager backup package.

To make a backup copy of your Business Contact Manager database:

1. Click Business Contact Manager | Database Tools | Manage Database.
2. In the Manage Database dialog box, Click the Back Up Database button.
3. Click the Browse button and specify a location and file name for the database backup package.
4. If you want, you can add a password. Be careful about this, though. If you add a password to the backup package, you'll need it to restore the database. If you forget the password, you'll be out of luck.
5. Click OK. The backup file will be generated. If your database is large, this could take some time.

Backed up Business Contact Manager databases are stored as .sbb files.

If you are working in a workgroup and require automated features like automated backup, you might be a good candidate to upgrade to ACT! by Sage (www.act.com). ACT! is the only major program in the same price range as Business Contact Manager, and it offers much more workgroup functionality.

Database Backup

To back up all of your linked items, you must also back up your Outlook data files.

Back up your database to:

[   ] Browse...

Optional password protection

Password: [   ]

Verify password: [   ]

Help   OK   Cancel

Task B Restoring your Business Contact Manager database

Restoring a Business Contact Manager database deletes your current Business Contact Manager database and overwrites it with the data contained in your backup package.

Read that last sentence again.

To restore a backed up Business Contact Manager database package:

1. Click Business Contact Manager | Database Tools | Manage Database.
2. In the Manage Database dialog box, Click the Restore Database button.
3. Click the Browse button and locate your database backup package.
4. If you added a password when creating the backup package, type it in the Password field.
5. Click OK. Your current database will be deleted and replaced with the version contained in the backup package.

Warning! When you restore a previously backed-up database, your current database is overwritten with the backup.

Database maintenance

From time to time, you should perform routine maintenance on your database. Think of the tasks in this section as an oil change for your database. Every once in a while, perform these simple tasks to avoid a database meltdown. You'll be glad you did.

Task A Checking a database for errors

If you suspect that your Business Contact Manager database is corrupt, you can check it for common errors. Any errors found will appear in the log that appears on the screen after performing the check.

If you use the database often, performing a weekly check is probably a good idea.

To check the Business Contact Manager database for errors:

1. Click Business Contact Manager | Database Tools | Manage Database.
2. Click the Check for Errors button.
3. Click Start. Business Contact Manager will defragment and check the database tables. Details of the check will appear in the Details section of the Check for Errors dialog box.
4. Click the Close button.

Task B	## Viewing a list of databases you can access

If you're wondering which databases are currently accessible from your computer, you can bring up a list of databases that you have previously connected to.

To view databases that you can currently access:

1. Click Business Contact Manager | Database Tools | Manage Database.
2. Click the Other Databases tab.
3. View the list of Business Contact Manager databases that you can currently access.

The current database does not show on the list of databases. You know you have access to this database because it's already open.

Manage Database

You can view information about this and other databases to which you have access, back up or restore the current database, and check the database for errors.

| | Backup/Restore | Other Databases |

Database Name	Size(MB)	Type	Owner	Created	
MSSmallBusines...	35	Offline copy ...	KACHINSKE\bcmuser	6/20/2007 9:...	
MSSmallBusines...	35	Offline copy ...	KACHINSKE\bcmuser	6/20/2007 9:...	
MSSmallBusines...	35	Offline copy ...	KACHINSKE\bcmuser	6/21/2007 6:...	

Delete Database

Help   Close

Task C   Deleting a database

Be careful about deleting a database. Following these instructions can only be done by a database creator or administrator, and once you delete a database, you can't easily recover the data.

To delete a database:

1. Click Business Contact Manager | Database Tools | Manage Database.
2. Click the Other Databases tab.
3. Highlight the Business Contact Manager database you would like to delete. Note that you cannot delete the currently open database. Your current database will not appear on this list.
4. Click the Delete Database button.
5. Click Yes to confirm the database's deletion.
6. Click Close.

It's probably a good idea to make a backup of the database before deleting it. Once you delete the database, you will not be able to retrieve any of the contacts in the database unless you have a backup.

Task D   Opening a database

When you have Outlook with Business Contact Manager open, you always have a database open. This database is referred to as your current database. If you want to open a different database, follow these steps.

To select the current database:

1. Click Business Contact Manager | Database Tools | Create or Select a Database.
2. Choose the Select an existing database option.
3. If the database you are trying to connect to is on a different computer, type the name of the computer in the Computer name field and click Connect. You may need to provide login credentials to access the other computer.
4. From the Database name drop-down, select a database and click Next.

You can only connect to one database at a time. If you want to see contacts from multiple databases at once, you'll have to import your second database's contacts into your master database.

Index

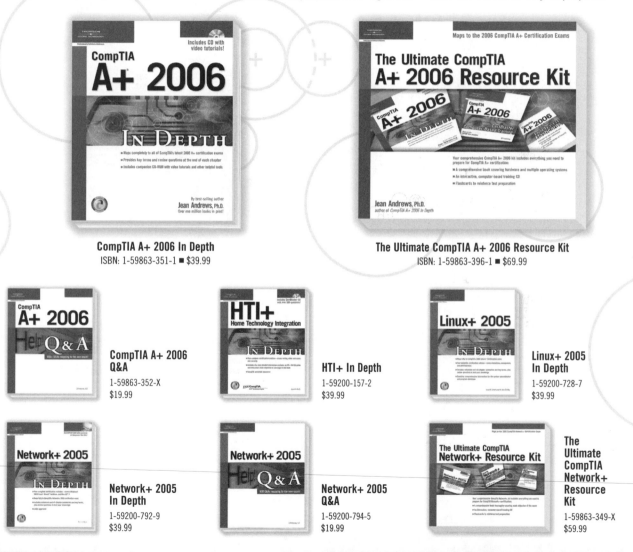